Series Adviser Cat...

Audio CD included

Navigate

Workbook
with key

Pre-intermediate → B1

OXFORD
UNIVERSITY PRESS

Contents

Oxford 3000™ *Navigate* has been based on the Oxford 3000 to ensure that learners are only covering the most relevant vocabulary.

1 Time — page 4

Grammar
- Question forms — 5
- Present simple and adverbs of frequency — 6

Vocabulary
- Daily life — 4
- Free-time activities — 7
- Nouns and verbs with the same form — 8
- Vocabulary review — 8

Speaking
- Talking about the weather — 9
- Talking about likes and dislikes — 9

Writing
- A web post about the best time to visit your country — 9

2 Inside outside — page 10

Grammar
- Present simple and present continuous — 11
- Identifying relative clauses — 12

Vocabulary
- Street life — 10
- Household objects — 13
- Phrases with *on* — 14
- Vocabulary review — 14

Speaking
- Asking for and giving directions — 15

Writing
- Text messages — 15

Reading for pleasure
- *Chemical Secret* – Pollution — 16

Review: Units 1 and 2 — 17

3 Going up, going down — page 18

Grammar
- Past simple — 19
- Past simple and past continuous — 21

Vocabulary
- Movement — 18
- Adjectives for describing feelings — 20
- Adverbs of manner — 22
- Vocabulary review — 22

Speaking
- Telling and responding to a story — 23

Writing
- Email (1): describing an event — 23

4 Changes and challenges — page 24

Grammar
- Verbs with *-ing* and *to* — 25
- *Going to* and present continuous for the future — 27

Vocabulary
- Life stages and events — 24
- Internet activities — 26
- *Get* — 28
- Vocabulary review — 28

Speaking
- Inviting and making arrangements — 29

Writing
- Email (2): making arrangements — 29

Listening for pleasure
- Ecological housing — 30

Review: Units 3 and 4 — 31

5 Stuff and things — page 32

Grammar
- Articles — 33
- Quantifiers — 35

Vocabulary
- Adjectives for describing objects — 32
- Money — 34
- Suffixes — 36
- Vocabulary review — 36

Speaking
- Explaining words you don't know — 37

Writing
- Email (3): returning an online product — 37

6 People — page 38

Grammar
- Making comparisons — 39
- Present perfect simple and past simple — 41

Vocabulary
- Adjectives for describing character — 38
- Family — 40
- Adjective prefixes — 42
- Vocabulary review — 42

Speaking
- Giving and responding to news — 43

Writing
- Responding to news on social media — 43

Reading for pleasure
- *Martin Luther King* – Little Rock — 44

Review: Units 5 and 6 — 45

7 Travel — page 46

Grammar
- Prediction (*will*, *might*) — 47
- *Something, anyone, everybody, nowhere*, etc — 49

Vocabulary
- Transport — 46
- Holidays — 48
- *-ed* and *-ing* adjectives — 50
- Vocabulary review — 50

Speaking
- Checking into a hotel — 51

Writing
- Short notes and messages — 51

8 Language and learning — page 52

Grammar
- Ability (*can, be able to*) — 52
- Obligation, necessity and permission (*must, have to, can*) — 55

Vocabulary
- Skills and abilities — 53
- Education — 54
- *Make* and *do* — 56
- Vocabulary review — 56

Speaking
- Asking for clarification — 57

Writing
- Completing a form — 57

Listening for pleasure
- Frightening experiences — 58

Review: Units 7 and 8 — 59

9 Body and mind — page 60

Grammar
- *If* + present simple, *will/won't/might* — 61
- Present tenses in future time clauses — 63

Vocabulary
- Body and actions — 60
- Health and fitness — 62
- Verbs and prepositions — 64
- Vocabulary review — 64

Speaking
- Asking for help and giving advice — 65

Writing
- A formal covering letter — 65

10 Food — page 66

Grammar
- Uses of the *-ing* form — 67
- The passive — 69

Vocabulary
- Describing food — 66
- Food containers — 68
- Words with more than one meaning — 70
- Vocabulary review — 70

Speaking
- Problems in a restaurant — 71

Writing
- A restaurant review — 71

Reading for pleasure
- *Chocolate* – Making chocolate — 72

Review: Units 9 and 10 — 73

11 World — page 74

Grammar
- *If* + past tense + *would* — 75
- *Used to* — 76

Vocabulary
- Global issues — 74
- The news — 77
- Phrasal verbs — 78
- Vocabulary review — 78

Speaking
- Expressing and responding to opinions — 79

Writing
- A presentation — 79

12 Work — page 80

Grammar
- Present perfect simple with *for* and *since* — 81
- Uses of the infinitive with *to* — 83

Vocabulary
- Jobs, professions and workplaces — 80
- Job responsibilities — 82
- Phrases with *in* — 84
- Vocabulary review — 84

Speaking
- Answering questions in a job interview — 85

Writing
- A curriculum vitae (CV) — 85

Listening for pleasure
- Easter Island statues — 86

Review: Units 11 and 12 — 87

Audioscripts — page 88

Answer key — page 94

1 Time

1.1 Do you live in the past, present or future?

Vocabulary daily life

1 What do you do? Match situations 1–8 to verb phrases a–h.

1 You need a holiday.
2 You go to a party.
3 It's raining.
4 Your boss arrives.
5 You're bored.
6 It's your cousin's birthday.
7 You're ill.
8 You have a busy weekend.

a spend time with relatives
b do some work
c eat healthy food and you'll feel better
d have fun
e make a to-do list
f stay in
g go on a trip
h chat with friends online

2 Complete the to-do list with the correct verbs.

THINGS TO DO

SATURDAY

1 _do_ housework
2 _____ the shopping (buy something for lunch!)
3 _____ some exercise (football 3 p.m.)
Go dancing – 4 _____ a good time!
5 _____ to bed late

SUNDAY

6 _____ a lie-in!
7 _____ a family meal
8 _____ future plans (holiday with family this year?)
9 _____ English homework
10 _____ an early night

3 Match verbs in A to phrases in B to make verb phrases. Then complete the information sheet.

A | do ~~eat~~ go go have have spend stay

B | an early night a good time ~~healthy food~~ in shopping some exercise time with relatives to bed late

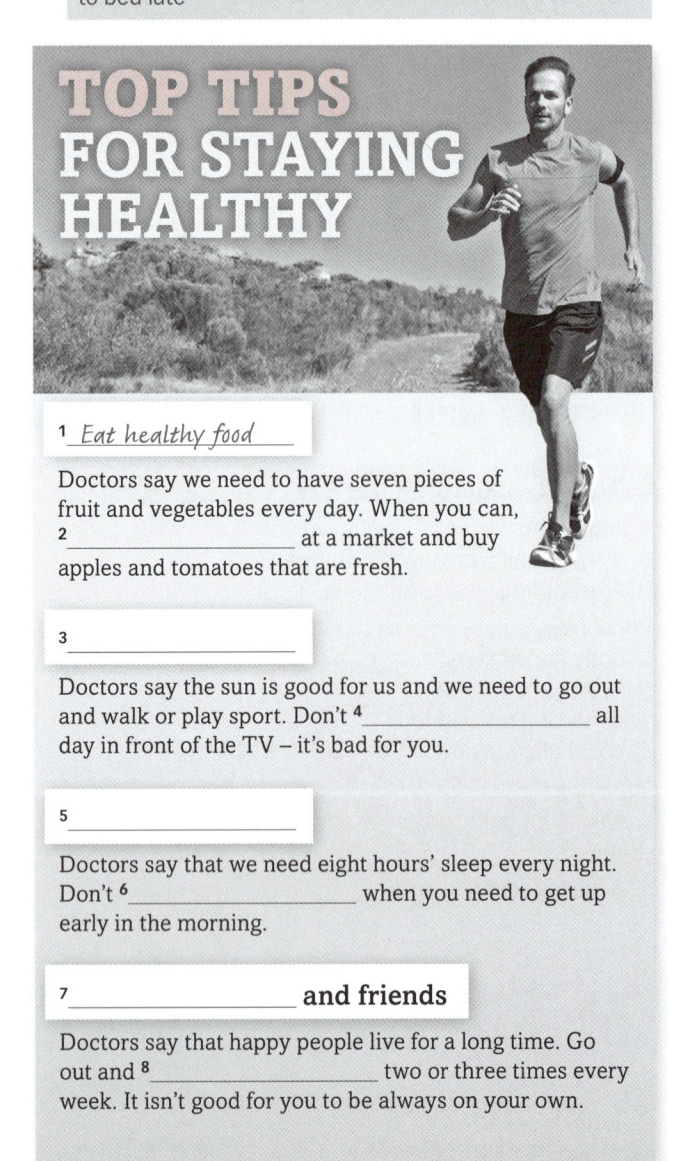

TOP TIPS FOR STAYING HEALTHY

1 _Eat healthy food_

Doctors say we need to have seven pieces of fruit and vegetables every day. When you can, 2 _____ at a market and buy apples and tomatoes that are fresh.

3 _____

Doctors say the sun is good for us and we need to go out and walk or play sport. Don't 4 _____ all day in front of the TV – it's bad for you.

5 _____

Doctors say that we need eight hours' sleep every night. Don't 6 _____ when you need to get up early in the morning.

7 _____ and friends

Doctors say that happy people live for a long time. Go out and 8 _____ two or three times every week. It isn't good for you to be always on your own.

4 | Oxford 3000™

Grammar question forms

4a Complete the conversations with the question words in the box.

> how many   how much   how often   what kind
> what time   when   where   who

1. **A** _What time_ do you get up during the week?
   B At half past seven.
2. **A** _____ is the first person you see every morning?
   B My brother. He gets up at the same time as me.
3. **A** _____ do you have breakfast?
   B In the kitchen.
4. **A** _____ coffee do you drink?
   B I have three or four cups a day.
5. **A** _____ do you stop for lunch?
   B From one o'clock until two.
6. **A** _____ do you eat in a restaurant?
   B About twice a month.
7. **A** _____ good friends do you have?
   B A lot. I have a lot of good friends.
8. **A** _____ of car do you drive?
   B I drive a Mini.

b 1.1 Listen and check.

c 1.1 Listen again. Pause the CD and repeat after each question.

5a Insert the word in brackets in the correct place in the sentences.
1. When your birthday? (is)   _When is your birthday?_
2. Who you chat with online? (do)
3. What kind films do you like? (of)
4. Are busy right now? (you)
5. How do you spend time with relatives? (often)
6. How many did you sleep last night? (hours)
7. Where you from? (are)
8. You go shopping yesterday? (did)

b 1.2 Listen and check.

c 1.2 Listen again. Pause the CD and repeat after each question.

6 Complete the questions in the conversation with question words and the verbs in brackets.

A Hi. It's nice to meet you. [1] _Are you_ (be) new?
B Yes, I am. My name's Laila.
A I'm Sally. [2] _____ _____ _____ (have) fun tonight?
B Yes, I did. It was a great class.
A [3] _____ _____ _____ _____ (start) playing tennis?
B Years ago. I was about ten, I think.
A [4] _____ _____ (be) good at it?
B Well … I won some competitions last year.
A How [5] _____ _____ _____ _____ (win)?
B Three or four.
A Congratulations! Laila, [6] _____ _____ _____ (live) near here?
B No, I live in the town centre.
A Me, too. [7] _____ _____ _____ _____ (get) here today?
B I came by bus.
A This is my car. [8] _____ _____ _____ (want) to go home together?
B Yes! Thanks a lot.
A No problem.

I can …	Very well	Quite well	More practice
talk about my daily life.	○	○	○
ask questions.	○	○	○

5

1.2 Free time

Grammar present simple and adverbs of frequency

1a Put the words in the right order to make sentences.
1 often / coffee / for / go / They / out / a
   They often go out for a coffee.
2 goes / My / and / running / then / every / girlfriend / now
   _____
3 don't / the / usually / We / camping / in / go / summer
   _____
4 best / aerobics / a / friend / My / twice / week / or / does / once
   _____
5 ever / games / I / play / hardly / computer
   _____
6 family / often / My / future / don't / plans / make
   _____

b 1.3))) Listen and check. Notice which words and parts of words are stressed.

c 1.3))) Listen again. Pause the CD and repeat after each word.

2 Complete the second sentence so that it means the same as the first. Replace the **bold** words with the adverbs and expressions in the box.

| ~~always~~   every now and then   most days |
| once or twice a year   rarely |

1 My partner does exercise after work **every day**.
   My partner *always does exercise* after work.
2 They **hardly ever** have a lie-in because they have two small children.
   They _____ because they have two small children.
3 My sister **nearly always** goes on Facebook before she has breakfast.
   _____ before she has breakfast.
4 My parents go on holiday **in January and July or only in July**.
   My parents _____.
5 We **occasionally** go clubbing with a big group of friends.
   _____ with a big group of friends.

3 Complete the article with the verb phrases and the adverbs in the box.

| always   ~~hardly ever~~   nearly always   never   occasionally |
| often   sometimes   usually |

	Mon	Tues	Weds	Thurs	Fri	Sat	Sun
eat healthily	✓	✓	✓	✓	✓	✓	✓
go training	✓	✓	✓	✓	✓	✓	
be in bed by 11 p.m.	✓	✓	✓	✓	✓		
chat with friends online	✓		✓		✓		✓
watch videos		✓		✓		✓	
spend time with relatives							✓
have a lie-in							✓
be bored							

A week in the life of an Olympic athlete

Olympic athletes have to look after their health if they want to be the best. In the morning, they ¹ *hardly ever have* a lie-in because they have a lot of things to do – a sports star ² _____ bored! In general, athletes ³ _____ and they start the day with a big breakfast with lots of carbohydrates and protein. They ⁴ _____ training in the morning and again in the evening. After training, they ⁵ _____ of other athletes to see how good they are. Olympic athletes don't have a lot of time to see other people, but they ⁶ _____ at the weekend – having a meal or catching up on family news. They ⁷ _____ or by phone. Professional athletes need between eight and ten hours sleep every night, so they ⁸ _____ in bed by 11 p.m.

Vocabulary — free-time activities

4 Write phrases for the photos with the words in the box and *play*, *do* or *go*.

aerobics ~~basketball~~ camping cards clubbing on Facebook to the gym yoga

1. play basketball
2.
3.
4.
5.
6.
7.
8.

5 Circle the incorrect phrase.
1. GO (aerobics) for a walk on Facebook running
2. PLAY basketball chess computer games swimming
3. DO exercise golf karate yoga
4. GO basketball camping out for a coffee to the gym
5. PLAY cards football golf karate
6. GO clubbing exercise out for a meal swimming

6 Complete the advert with *play*, *do* or *go* and the words and phrases in the box.

~~computer games~~ exercise football for a meal for a walk golf running swimming

CenterParcs

Looking for a perfect family holiday?

CenterParcs is not the place to go if you want to ¹ *play computer games* all day. But it **is** right for you if you're looking for some action! Here are some of the exciting activities you can do:

▸ ² _____ in the outdoor pool. The pool is heated to 29.5°C so it isn't cold.

▸ ³ _____ in our fitness classes. There are Zumba classes for all the family!

▸ ⁴ _____ on our 18-hole course. You're sure to have a good time.

▸ ⁵ _____ in the forest and learn more about nature. If you have more energy, you can ⁶ _____ early in the morning when everybody is asleep.

▸ send your children to ⁷ _____. Our coach will teach them for an hour before they play a match together.

▸ after all the excitement, ⁸ _____ in one of our many restaurants. It's a great time to relax!

To find out more information on CenterParcs, check out their website.

I can …	Very well	Quite well	More practice
talk about how often I do things.	○	○	○
talk about my free time.	○	○	○

1.3 Vocabulary development

Vocabulary nouns and verbs with the same form

1 Complete the conversations with the words in the box. Use the correct form of the same word for each conversation.

> dream experience ~~photograph~~ plan post
> promise text

1. A Do you take many _photographs_ ?
   B No, I only _photograph_ things that interest me.
2. A Who do you tell first if you have a bad _____ ?
   B If I _____ something awful, I always tell my best friend.
3. A Do you make a _____ for the week every Monday morning?
   B Yes, I _____ exactly what I'm going to do.
4. A Do you often have the same _____ every night?
   B Yes, I _____ that I am falling into a dark hole.
5. A Do you usually call your friends or do you write a _____ ?
   B I always _____ them before we go out.
6. A Do you always think hard before you make a _____ ?
   B No. I often _____ to phone my parents and then I forget.
7. A Do you often write _____ on Facebook?
   B No, but I often _____ music videos.

2 Complete the article with the correct form of some of the words in exercise 1.

> Mobile phones can do more things today than ever before. Of course, you can use them to make calls and write [1] _texts_ , but they are also great for taking [2] _____ . A phone camera is better than a digital camera because it is always with you. You don't usually [3] _____ to photograph something when you leave home, but if you see something interesting or have an unusual [4] _____ , you can take out your phone and [5] _____ it. Today, you can also have more fun with your photos. In the past, you put a photo on your computer, and you hardly ever had a look at it again. But now, you can go on Facebook and [6] _____ your photos on your profile. You can also publish them on a blog. With all of this new technology, we can do things that people didn't [7] _____ of in the past.

Vocabulary review

→ **STUDY TIP** When you come across new verb phrases, record them under the verb in your notebooks. This will make it easier for you to learn them.

3 Complete the table with the phrases in the box.

> ~~a family meal~~ a good time a lie-in a to-do list
> an early night fun future plans healthy food
> homework housework in on a trip shopping
> some exercise some work the shopping
> time with relatives to bed late with friends online

chat	do	eat	go

have	make	spend	stay
a family meal			

4 Complete the table with the headings in the box.

> do go play

1_____	2_____	3_____
camping	cards	aerobics
clubbing	chess	exercise
for a walk	computer games	karate
on Facebook	football	yoga
out for coffee/a meal	golf	
running	basketball	
swimming		
to the gym		

5 Complete the table with the correct headings.

1_____	2_____	3_____
a look	a photograph	a film
an experience		a record
a dream		a promise

1.4 Speaking and writing

Speaking talking about the weather

1 Complete the conversation with the words in the box.

~~damp~~ humid mild pleasant showers thunderstorm

A What's the weather like where you are?
B It's raining today, so everything is ¹ _damp_ .
A Does it rain a lot in your area?
B It doesn't usually rain all day, but we often have a few ² _____ .
A What's it like in the summer?
B It isn't very ³ _____ , because it gets very hot and ⁴ _____ . Occasionally, there's a ⁵ _____ in the evening, which can be quite frightening.
A What's your favourite season?
B I like the spring. It's nearly always very ⁶ _____ , and you can go out without a coat.

Speaking talking about likes and dislikes

2a Complete the second sentence so that it means the same as the first, using the word in brackets.
1 I like going clubbing a lot. (love)
   I _love going clubbing._
2 I hate the winter. (stand)
   I _____
3 I like doing yoga a lot. (into)
   I _____
4 I like basketball more than any other sport. (favourite)
   My _____
5 Doing housework isn't a problem for me. (mind)
   I _____
6 I don't like thunderstorms. (keen)
   I _____
7 Going camping is OK, I suppose. (quite)
   I _____
8 I like football more than golf. (prefer)
   I _____
9 I like doing karate a lot. (interested)
   I _____

PRONUNCIATION sentence stress

b 1.4))) Listen and check. Notice which words and parts of the words are stressed.

c 1.4))) Listen again. Pause the CD and repeat after each word.

Writing a web post about the best time to visit your country

3 Complete the web post with *and*, *but* or *so*.

Suzanne Fischer

My family and I would like to visit Rio de Janeiro, Brazil. When is the best time to go?

Paulo

The most popular time to visit Rio is from December to March. This is our summer season ¹ _but_ it sometimes rains. The weather is usually nice and warm, ² _____ the sun can be very dangerous. You need to use cream when you go outside ³ _____ it's safer to stay inside in the middle of the day.

The city is always busy in the summer ⁴ _____ it can be very expensive. ⁵ _____ the best time to come is in spring or autumn when flights are cheaper ⁶ _____ there are fewer tourists.

Have a good trip!

I can …	Very well	Quite well	More practice
understand and use nouns and verbs with the same form.	○	○	○
talk about the weather, my likes and dislikes.	○	○	○
write a web post.	○	○	○

2 Inside outside

2.1 Street life

Vocabulary street life

1 Choose the correct option to complete the sentences.
1 Ellis Island isn't *dirty / huge / safe*, but there's an important statue on it.
2 The bus is *crowded / dull / safe*. There are a lot of passengers.
3 It's a *dirty / dull / lively* market. There are a lot of stalls.
4 The beach is *crowded / huge / safe*. You can swim in the sea.
5 The park is *dirty / huge / lively*. There's a lot of rubbish.
6 It's a *crowded / dull / lively* area. There's nothing to do.

2 Match words in column A to words in column B to make compound nouns. Then match the compound nouns to the definitions 1–7.

A	B
street	area
parking	cleaner
souvenir	artist
pavement	performer
market	place
pedestrian	space
street	seller

1 A person who picks up the rubbish. *street cleaner*
2 A place where cars can't go. _____
3 A person who has a stall with things for tourists. _____
4 A place where there are a lot of stalls. _____
5 A person who draws pictures on the street. _____
6 A place where you can leave your car. _____
7 A person who acts or sings outside. _____

3 Complete the article with the words in exercises 1 and 2.

Famous city squares

Djemaa el Fna is a ¹ *lively* square full of energy in the centre of Marrakech in Morocco. This is a ² _____ _____ with no cars, so the best way to go there is on foot. During the day, the square is a ³ _____ _____ where people go shopping. There are all kinds of ⁴ _____, selling everything from carpets to spices. You can see ⁵ _____ _____, such as dancers and story tellers, and you can buy presents to take home from the ⁶ _____ _____. The market fills all the narrow streets around the square, so it is absolutely ⁷ _____. The busiest time of day is late afternoon when the market is very ⁸ _____. The square is quite ⁹ _____ as there are police officers on every corner. At the end of the evening, the square is very ¹⁰ _____ and there is a lot of ¹¹ _____ on the streets. In the early morning, it's time for the ¹² _____ _____ to start work and prepare the square for the next day.

PRONUNCIATION word stress in street life words

4a Underline the syllable we stress in these words.
1 cleaner
2 crowded
3 lively
4 market
5 pavement
6 pedestrian
7 performer
8 rubbish
9 souvenir
10 statue

b 2.1))) Listen and check.

c 2.1))) Listen again. Pause the CD and repeat after each word.

Grammar present simple and present continuous

5a Complete the sentences with the present continuous form of the verbs in the box. Use contractions where possible.

celebrate do not feel ~~have~~ run not talk wait not watch

1 We're tired. We'_re having_ an early night.
2 My husband is late for work. He _____ out of the door.
3 You can turn the TV off. I _____ it.
4 Your dog is hungry. It _____ by the cupboard.
5 Can you help me? I _____ my English homework.
6 My parents are angry. They _____ to each other.
7 Robert is in bed. He _____ very well.
8 My grandfather is 80 today. We _____ his birthday with him.

PRONUNCIATION contractions in present continuous

b 2.2))) Listen and check.

c 2.2))) Listen again. Pause the CD and repeat after each word.

6 Choose the correct options to complete the conversations.
1 A Where *do you go / are you going*?
   B To the shops. *Do you want / Are you wanting* anything?
2 A *Do you listen / Are you listening* to the radio at the moment?
   B Yes, I *like / 'm liking* this programme.
3 A What *do you do / are you doing* on Saturday evenings?
   B I usually *go / 'm going* out.
4 A What time *does the market open / is the market opening*?
   B I *don't know / 'm not knowing*, sorry.
5 A *Does your partner / Is your partner* working today?
   B No, he *doesn't work / isn't working* on Fridays.
6 A *Do you have / Are you having* fun?
   B Yes, I *have / 'm having* a great time.
7 A *Do I need / Am I needing* an umbrella?
   B No, it *doesn't rain / isn't raining*.
8 A *Is our team winning / Does our team win*?
   B No, they *play / 're playing* really badly today.

7 Rewrite the sentences with the correct time expression in brackets.
1 I make a to-do list. (never/nowadays)
   I never make a to-do list.
2 My parents have a family meal. (every Sunday/now)
   _____
3 We're eating healthy food. (usually/these days)
   _____
4 My partner is doing some work. (occasionally/at the moment)
   _____
5 Luca goes to bed late. (always/now)
   _____
6 I'm chatting with friends online. (often/right now)
   _____

8 Complete the article with the correct present simple or present continuous form of the verbs in brackets.

Fabulous La Rambla

One of the most famous streets in the world is La Rambla in Barcelona, Spain. La Rambla ¹_starts_ (start) in the Plaça de Catalunya, a huge square in the centre of the city, and ²_____ (finish) at the statue of Christopher Columbus in the port. The street ³_____ (have) a central pedestrian area and it ⁴_____ (get) very crowded at the weekend.

Today is a typical day in La Rambla and the street is full of tourists. Some people ⁵_____ (sit) at pavement cafés and others ⁶_____ (watch) the street performers. A local woman ⁷_____ (buy) some flowers from a stall and an American tourist ⁸_____ (look) at postcards at a souvenir seller's. He ⁹_____ (want) to write to his friends back home.

Most people ¹⁰_____ (like) going to La Rambla because there is so much to do and see there, and it ¹¹_____ (become) one of the most important parts of Barcelona. These days more tourists ¹²_____ (spend) time there than ever before.

I can …	Very well	Quite well	More practice
talk about where I live.	○	○	○
talk about the present.	○	○	○

11

2.2 Home life

Grammar identifying relative clauses

1 Choose the correct options to complete the article.

Making igloos

The Inuit are a group of people ¹(that) / where / which live north of the Arctic Circle. Nunavut is the name of the area ²where / which / who they live in Canada. It is a place ³where / which / who the temperature often goes down to -40°C. The Inuit sometimes build igloos to protect themselves from the cold when they are hunting animals. An igloo is a round house ⁴that / where / who is made out of snow. There are Inuits ⁵where / which / who can build an igloo in less than an hour. They use snow ⁶where / which / who is very hard, and they cut it into squares. Inside an igloo, it can be 16°C when it is well below freezing outside.

2a Complete the definitions with *where*, *which* or *who*. Then match them to the words in the box.

ball dentist DVD garage kitchen ~~neighbour~~ picture police officer

1 It's a person _who_ lives in the house next to you. _neighbour_
2 It's the place _____ you keep your car. _____
3 It's a thing _____ you put on the wall. _____
4 It's a thing _____ you watch when there's nothing on TV. _____
5 It's the person _____ looks after your teeth. _____
6 It's a thing _____ you use to do sport. _____
7 It's the place _____ you make lunch. _____
8 It's a person _____ keeps you safe. _____

b In which sentences in exercise **2a** could *where*, *which* or *who* be replaced by *that*?

3 Join the two sentences to make one sentence. Use *where*, *which* or *who*.
1 They're shoes. I wear them to go running.
  They're the shoes _which I wear to go running._
2 That's a phone. I use it for work.
  That's the phone _____
3 He's a mechanic. He repairs my car.
  He's the mechanic _____
4 That's a chair. My grandfather always sits there.
  That's the chair _____
5 She's a hairdresser. She cuts my hair.
  She's the hairdresser _____
6 That's a bus. It goes to the city centre.
  That's the bus _____
7 That's a supermarket. We do our shopping there.
  That's the supermarket _____

PRONUNCIATION stress in relative clauses

4a Underline the words that are stressed.
1 It's something that you have in your house.
2 It's something that you turn on and off.
3 It's something that has water in it.

b 2.3))) Listen and check.

c 2.3))) Listen again. Pause the CD and repeat after each word.

Vocabulary household objects

5 Match words in box A to words in box B to make household objects. Then complete the sentences.

A	chest dish dustpan microwave satellite wash
B	basin and brush of drawers oven TV washer

1 A _dishwasher_ is a machine that cleans dirty plates and glasses.
2 A _____ _____ _____ are things that you use to clean the floor with.
3 The place where you usually clean your teeth is the _____ _____.
4 A machine where you can make food hot again is a _____ _____.
5 _____ _____ lets people watch programmes from all over the world.
6 The place where you keep some of your clothes is a _____ _____ _____.

6 Complete the crossword by looking at the photos.

(Crossword: 1 down = CARPET)

7 Complete the sentences with some of the words in exercises **5** and **6**.

1 Your hair looks awful. Look in the _mirror_.
2 The _____ is dirty because of your shoes. Please take them off.
3 I want to have a shower. Can I borrow a _____?
4 Your shirts are clean. Please hang them up in the _____.
5 I dropped my toast. Where can I find a _____?
6 The meal was delicious. Let me put the plates in the _____ for you.

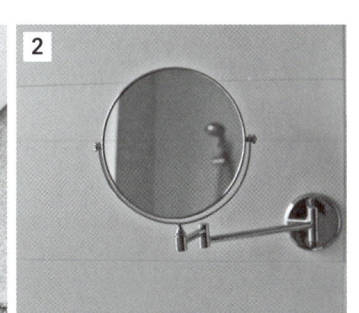

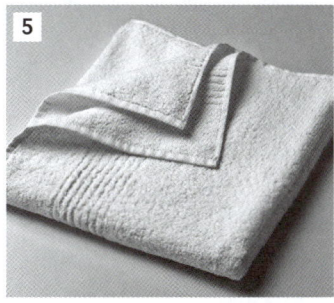

I can …

	Very well	Quite well	More practice
identify things and people.	○	○	○
talk about things in my home.	○	○	○

13

2.3 Vocabulary development

Vocabulary phrases with *on*

1 Match definitions 1–8 to phrases in the box.

> on business   on holiday   on public transport   on the internet
> on the left   on the way   on time   on TV

1 online _on the internet_
2 during the journey _____
3 opposite direction to 'on the right' _____
4 at the beach _____
5 you can watch it on the television _____
6 not late _____
7 on the metro, on a bus or on a tram _____
8 doing work activities _____

2 Complete the conversations with the phrases with *on* in exercise **1**.

1 A Can you buy some bread _on the way_ home?
   B Yes, of course. No problem.
2 A Where's your partner?
   B He's away _____. He has an important meeting in Brussels.
3 A How do I get to your house?
   B Walk down Princess Street towards the church and it's _____.
4 A Do you want to go by car?
   B No. Let's go _____. It's quicker.
5 A Aren't your parents at home?
   B No, they're _____ in Majorca.

Vocabulary review

3 Complete the table with the words in the box.

> crowded   market place   pavement artist   safe   statue
> street performer

Adjectives to describe your town	People in the street	Places and things in the street
1 _crowded_	3 _____	5 _____
dirty	souvenir seller	parking space
dull	street cleaner	pedestrian area
huge	4 _____	rubbish
lively		stall
2 _____		6 _____

STUDY TIP When you can, try to record new vocabulary in groups. A mind map is a great way of doing this and the new words will be easier to learn.

4 Complete the mind map with the headings in the box.

> things in the kitchen   things to clean with
> things in the bedroom   things in the sitting room
> things to light when it gets dark   things in the bathroom

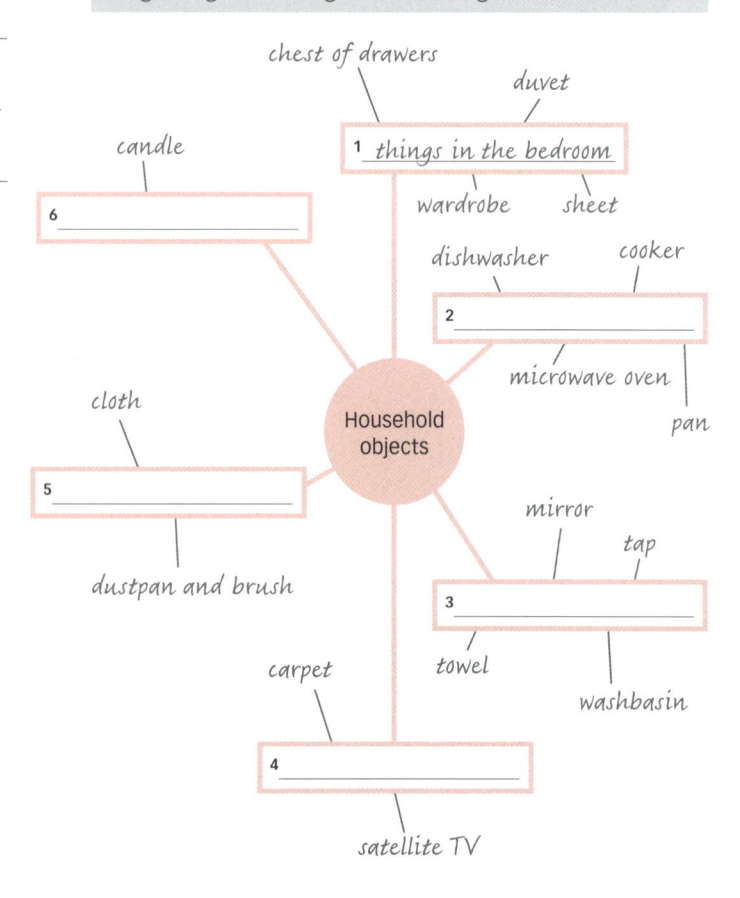

chest of drawers *duvet*
candle   1 _things in the bedroom_
wardrobe   *sheet*
6 _____
dishwasher   *cooker*
2 _____
microwave oven
cloth   **Household objects**   *pan*
5 _____
mirror
dustpan and brush   *tap*
3 _____
carpet   *towel*
washbasin
4 _____
satellite TV

5 Complete the table with the phrases in the box.

> on the way   checking news and information on the computer
> on business   positioned on the right-hand side

Phrases with *on*	Definition
on the internet	1 _checking news and information on the computer_
2 _____	for work reasons
on the right	3 _____
4 _____	travelling towards

14 Oxford 3000™

| | | 2.1 | 2.2 | **2.3** | **2.4** | 2.5 |

2.4 Speaking and writing

Speaking asking for and giving directions

1a Put the conversation in the right order 1–7.
___ Can you show us on the map?
___ Thanks.
___ That's right. It takes about ten minutes.
_1_ Please could you tell us how to get to the town hall?
___ Yes, here it is. You can't miss it.
___ Yes, go straight down here, cross the road at the lights and take the second left.
___ OK, so it's down here and second left after the lights?

b 2.4))) Listen and check.

2 Choose the correct option to complete the sentences.

A Erm, I ¹*'m looking* / *look* for the canteen.
B Yes, it's ² *on* / *in* the ground floor.
A Is it ³ *far* / *further*?
B No, not really. It's five minutes' ⁴ *walk* / *walking* from here.
A How do I get there?
B Go along the corridor, and ⁵ *take* / *turn* right at the end. Go down the ⁶ *stair* / *stairs* and you'll ⁷ *see* / *watch* the canteen in front of you.
A OK, so ⁸ *it's* / *there's* along here, right and down the stairs?
B That's right.
A Thanks.

3 Complete the conversation with the phrases in the box.

a lot   I need to go   is this the right way   on the left
that right   the first right   through the doors
until you reach

A Excuse me, ¹ _is this the right way_ to the bathroom?
B Yes, keep going ² _____ the double doors. Go ³ _____ and take ⁴ _____.
A So ⁵ _____ through the double doors and turn right. Is ⁶ _____?
B Yes. It's the door ⁷ _____.
A Thanks ⁸ _____.

Writing text messages

4 Rewrite the text messages using abbreviations.

> Hi! Where ¹ *are you*? Am waiting outside cinema. ² *See you* soon? ³ *Love Rachel*.

> ⁴ *Great!* ⁵ *Sorry* I'm late. Be there ⁶ *as soon as possible*. ⁷ *Please* could ⁸ *you* get tickets? ⁹ *Thanks!*

> Hi! Where ¹ _RU_ ? Am waiting outside cinema. ² _____ soon? ³ _____

> ⁴ _____ ! ⁵ _____ I'm late. Be there ⁶ _____ . ⁷ _____ could ⁸ _____ get tickets? ⁹ _____ !

I can …	Very well	Quite well	More practice
use phrases with *on*.	○	○	○
ask for and give directions.	○	○	○
write text messages.	○	○	○

15

2.5 Reading for pleasure

Pollution

1 Look at the photo. What kind of pollution does it show? Circle the correct answer 1, 2, 3 or 4.

1 air pollution 3 water pollution
2 noise pollution 4 land pollution

2 Read an extract from a short story called *Chemical Secret*.

3 Put the extract summary in the correct order 1–7.

___ John arrives in David Wilson's office.
___ David Wilson reads the report.
___ John says he's worried about the effects of the waste products.
___ Wilson says he doesn't like the conclusions in the report.
_1_ John does experiments to find out the effects of the waste products on rats and writes a report.
___ Wilson says he doesn't want to build new machines to clean up the waste products.
___ John gets very nervous and drinks water.

The story so far
John Duncan starts working in a factory. A few months later, he writes a report for his boss, David Wilson. Wilson calls John into his office to talk to him.

The report

'I've read your report,' Wilson began. Then he stopped. 'Not very good, is it?'

'What?' John stared at him in surprise.

Wilson smiled. 'No, no, don't worry – I don't mean the report is bad, of course not. You've worked very hard, and done your job well. What I mean is, I don't like the ideas at the end of the report.'

'What's wrong with them?'

'They're too expensive.' The two men stared at each other for a moment, and John felt cold and sick in his stomach. Wilson smiled, but it wasn't the kind of smile that John liked.

'Look, John,' he said. 'Your report says that we should build some new machines to clean up the waste products before they go into the river, right? And those machines will cost *two million pounds!* Where do you think we can find all that? Money doesn't grow on trees, you know!'

'No, of course not.' John's mouth was dry. He took a drink of water, and felt his hand shaking. 'But we're selling a lot of new paint. We're making millions of pounds every month from that, aren't we?'

'We're doing very well, yes,' said Wilson. 'But if we spend two million pounds to build these new machines, the paint will have to cost more, and we won't sell so much.'

'But – we've got to do it,' said John. 'These waste products are much more dangerous than I'd thought. Didn't you read that in my report? When I put the chemicals in rats' drinking water, some of the baby rats were born without eyes and ears. One didn't have any legs, and one had six.' He shivered. 'And some were born without legs when they drank only two parts per million. We can't put those chemicals in the river.'

Text extract from *Oxford Bookworms Factfiles: Chemical Secret*

4 Think about the events in the story.

Why do you think David Wilson doesn't want to spend money on the machines? Is it possible this kind of water pollution could happen in your country? Why/Why not?

Review: Units 1 and 2

Grammar

1 Complete the sentences with one word only.
   1 She usually goes clubbing with some friends _who_ love dancing.
   2 I do exercise _____ or twice a week.
   3 What _____ of car do you drive?
   4 He's driving _____ the moment so he can't talk on the phone.
   5 My parents go on a trip _____ month.
   6 How _____ do you have a family meal?

2 Choose the correct options to complete the advert.

Why not take a **trip** down the **Nile**?

¹ *Do you make* / *Are you making* plans now for your next summer holiday? If you ² *want* / *are wanting* a trip with a difference, why not try a cruise down the River Nile? Our boat ³ *leaves* / *is leaving* from Luxor every Monday morning and we ⁴ *don't arrive* / *aren't arriving* at our first stop until the next day. The trip ⁵ *lasts* / *is lasting* for seven nights and right now we ⁶ *offer* / *are offering* a special price. Just think what the guests ⁷ *do* / *are doing* right now! If you ⁸ *look* / *are looking* for a little adventure in your life, a Nile cruise is the trip for you. You're sure to have a lot of fun!

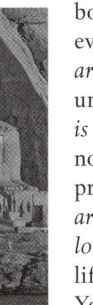

Vocabulary

3 Match definitions 1-8 to words and phrases in the box.

   dishwasher   do aerobics   do housework
   go out for a meal   have a lie-in   lively   stall   ~~towel~~

   1 a thing you use to dry yourself   _towel_
   2 get up late   _____
   3 a shop with an open front   _____
   4 do exercise to music   _____
   5 a machine that cleans plates, glasses, etc. _____
   6 very exciting   _____
   7 clean the flat   _____
   8 have dinner in a restaurant   _____

4 Complete the words in the text.

One of the largest cities in the world is Shanghai in China. The city is on the River Yangtze on the east coast and it's absolutely ¹ h_uge_ – more than 23 million people live there. Houses are expensive because the city is so ² cr_____, and most people live in very small flats. There isn't much room inside, so families don't often ³ st_____ in when they have free time. In the evenings, they go and sit outside: the adults on chairs and the children on a ⁴ r_____. Here they play ⁵ ch_____ together, tell stories or just ⁶ ch_____ with their friends. In the summer, it's too hot to go to bed so nobody has an ⁷ e_____ night.

5 Match words from A to words from B to form phrases. Then complete the sentences with the phrases.

   A   have   ~~on~~   on   on   make   take

   B   a dream   ~~holiday~~   a photograph   a promise
       public transport   time

   1 My neighbours aren't at home. They're _on holiday_.
   2 I can't get to work _____. I have to take my car.
   3 I often _____ about the house where I lived as a child.
   4 When you get married you have to _____ to look after your partner.
   5 You're always late. You're never _____.
   6 We can't show you our hotel because we didn't _____ of it.

Speaking

6 Complete the conversations with the phrases in the box.

   Go straight down   I'm really   ~~I prefer~~   it's five minutes' walk

   1 A What's your favourite season – summer or winter?
      B _I prefer_ summer to winter.
   2 A Please could you tell me how to get to the sports centre?
      B Sure. _____ the road and turn left.
   3 A Is it far to the park?
      B No, _____ from here.
   4 A Which sport do you like best?
      B _____ into basketball.

17

3 Going up, going down

3.1 The man who fell to Earth

Vocabulary movement

1 Match definitions 1–9 to verbs in the box.

climb dive drop fall jump land lift rise take off

1 drop down towards the ground — *fall*
2 move upwards — _____
3 come down from the air — _____
4 leave the ground and start flying — _____
5 move higher using your hands and feet — _____
6 let something fall — _____
7 move something up to a higher position — _____
8 jump into the water with your arms and head first — _____
9 move quickly into the air by pushing yourself up with your legs and feet — _____

2 Choose the correct option to complete the sentences.
1 The wall wasn't very high, so my brother jumped *along / (over) / towards* it.
2 Walk *backwards / forward / towards* the main square and the restaurant is on the left.
3 We all got *out of / over / through* the car when we arrived.
4 I went *along / into / round and round* the room and sat down opposite the interviewer.
5 It's quicker to go *forward / out of / through* the park, if it's open.
6 They couldn't turn the car around, so they had to drive *backwards / forwards / towards* down the track.
7 She can't decide what to do. She keeps going *into / round and round / out of* in circles.
8 They went for a pleasant walk *along / into / through* the path by the river.

3 Complete the information sheet with the prepositions in the box.

along backwards forward into out of over through towards

HOW TO STAY SAFE IN THE COUNTRY: BULLS

In general, try to keep away from bulls if you can. If you have to go ¹ *into* a field where there is a bull, you need to be careful. Stay ² _____ the side of the field by the wall and don't try to run ³ _____ the middle. If the bull is looking at you, stop walking and don't move ⁴ _____ until it looks away again. If it starts making a noise and touching the ground with its foot, you need to get ⁵ _____ the field as soon as possible. Slowly walk ⁶ _____, and then climb ⁷ _____ the nearest wall. Then, if the bull comes ⁸ _____ you, you will already be safe.

Grammar past simple

→ **STUDY TIP** There is a list of irregular verbs on p.166 of your Student's Book. Study the infinitive and past simple of five verbs every day so you can remember them easily. This will make it easier for you to use the past simple correctly.

4 Write sentences in the past simple using the words in brackets.

1. The plane from Madrid lands at 22.40. (night)
   The plane from Madrid landed at 22.40 last night.
2. The sun rises every morning. (two hours)
   _____
3. Do you go on holiday every year? (the summer)
   _____
4. We have a family meal every weekend. (day before yesterday)
   _____
5. I don't climb trees. (I was young)
   _____
6. My friends go clubbing. (three days)
   _____
7. Do you spend time with relatives? (other day)
   _____
8. We don't do housework during the week. (Tuesday)
   _____

PRONUNCIATION regular past verbs

5a Underline the regular past simple form which has an extra syllable when you say the words.

1. dived   dropped   jumped   <u>landed</u>
2. booked   climbed   lifted   walked
3. arrived   travelled   turned   wanted
4. asked   looked   waited   worked
5. called   painted   played   listened
6. danced   helped   started   watched

b 3.1))) Listen and check.

c 3.1))) Listen again. Pause the CD and repeat after each word.

6 Complete the article with the correct past simple form of the verbs in brackets.

The first man in space

On 12th April 1961, Yuri Gagarin ¹ *became* (become) the first man to travel into outer space. At 6.07 a.m. he ² _____ (take off) in his spacecraft, Vostok 1, and then he ³ _____ (fly) once around the Earth. Nearly two hours later, he ⁴ _____ (parachute) down towards the ground, but he ⁵ _____ (not land) in the right place. He ⁶ _____ (finish) his trip in a field 280 km away. A farmer and his daughter ⁷ _____ (see) him land, and at first they ⁸ _____ (be) very frightened. Gagarin was a hero when he ⁹ _____ (return) to Earth, but he ¹⁰ _____ (not retire) from work. Instead, he ¹¹ _____ (travel) around the world telling his story. After that, he ¹² _____ (work) for the Russian Air Force and he ¹³ _____ (help) to test new planes. Unfortunately, one of Gagarin's planes ¹⁴ _____ (crash) on 27th March 1968 and he ¹⁵ _____ (die) in the accident at the age of 34.

I can …	Very well	Quite well	More practice
describe movement.	○	○	○
talk about the past (1).	○	○	○

19

3.2 Going up ... One man's lift nightmare

Vocabulary adjectives for describing feelings

1a Complete the sentences with words in the box.

> <u>angry</u> anxious calm confused disappointed
> embarrassed ~~excited~~ exhausted guilty lonely
> nervous pleased scared stressed

1 We're _excited_ because we're going on holiday tomorrow.
2 My mother was _____ because we were late for dinner.
3 I'm _____ because I don't remember your name.
4 He felt _____ because he made his little sister cry.
5 They're _____ because they've got an exam tomorrow.
6 My cousin is _____ because he failed his driving test again.
7 My sister is _____ because she can't understand the instructions.
8 I feel _____ because I did yoga this morning.
9 She's _____ because she hasn't got any friends.
10 He feels _____ because it's late and his daughter isn't home.
11 I'm _____ because my job interview went well.

PRONUNCIATION adjective word stress (1)

b <u>Underline</u> the syllable we stress in the adjectives in exercise 1a. Then complete the table.

One syllable	Two syllables	Three syllables	Four syllables
_____	_angry_	_____	_____
_____	_____	_____	_____
_____	_____	_____	
	_____	_____	
		_____	

c 3.2))) Listen and check.

d 3.2))) Listen again. Pause the CD and repeat after each word.

2a Use the words in exercise **1a** to complete the puzzle.

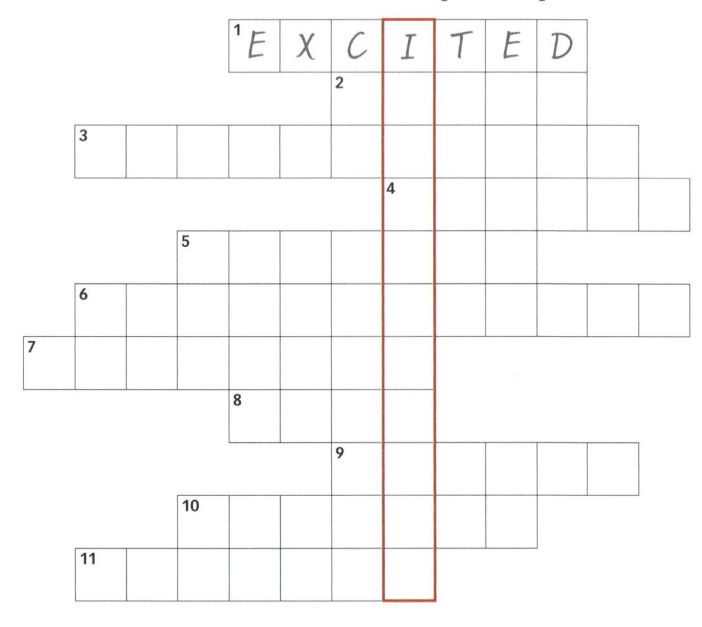

(Crossword: 1 across = EXCITED)

b What is the missing feeling?

Grammar past simple and past continuous

3 Complete the sentences with the past continuous form of the verb in brackets.
1 It _was raining_ (rain) when we left the house.
2 The children _____ (sleep) when we got home.
3 My partner didn't call because his mobile phone _____ (not work).
4 What _____ you _____ (talk) about when I came in?
5 Who _____ (drive) when the accident happened?
6 You _____ (not watch) the TV so I turned it off.
7 I _____ (live) in Paris when I met my husband.
8 We _____ (dance) when the lights went out.

4 Write sentences with *when*. Use the past simple and the past continuous.
1 I / drop a glass / I / do the washing up
 I dropped a glass when I was doing the washing up.
2 we / study in the library / the fire / start
 _____
3 my partner / break his leg / he / play football
 _____
4 a thief / take my bag / I / sit in the park
 _____
5 you / come out of the supermarket / I / see you
 _____
6 my friends / wait outside the cinema / I / arrive
 _____

5 Complete the article with the past simple or past continuous form of the verb in brackets.

GARDEN CHAIR PILOT

When Larry Walters was a teenager, he ¹ _saw_ (see) some balloons while he ² _____ (do) the shopping one day. He ³ _____ (think) about using them to fly, but he ⁴ _____ (not try) the idea until twenty years later. He ⁵ _____ (ask) his girlfriend and a friend to tie 45 balloons to a garden chair which he ⁶ _____ (sit) in. Then, they ⁷ _____ (fill) the balloons with helium. Immediately, Larry ⁸ _____ (rise) to a height of 3,600 m and he was very frightened. Then he noticed that the chair ⁹ _____ (go) towards Los Angeles Airport. Fortunately, he ¹⁰ _____ (come) down three-quarters of an hour later – before he reached the airport.

I can …	Very well	Quite well	More practice
talk about feelings.	○	○	○
talk about the past (2).	○	○	○

3.3 Vocabulary development

Vocabulary | adverbs of manner

1 Rewrite the sentences with verb + adverb.

1 They're bad tennis players.
   They play tennis badly.
2 He's a slow reader.
   _____
3 We're healthy eaters.
   _____
4 My mother is a fast walker.
   _____
5 I'm a careful driver.
   _____
6 You're a good cook.
   _____
7 My partner is a hard worker.
   _____
8 My brother is a smart dresser.
   _____

2 Complete the sentences with the adverb form of the adjectives in the box.

| beautiful easy fluent polite quick quiet ~~regular~~ |

1 My sister goes on business *regularly*. She's hardly ever at home.
2 Can you talk _____ please? I'm trying to read.
3 I used my GPS, so I found your house _____.
4 That girl has a lovely voice. She sings _____.
5 My partner lived in Berlin when he was young, so he speaks German _____.
6 Walk _____! We're going to be late!
7 She smiled _____ when I said hello, but I don't think she recognized me.

Vocabulary review

3 Complete the table with the headings in the box.

| going down   going up |

1 _____	2 _____
climb	dive
jump	drop
lift	fall
rise	jump
take off	land

4 Complete the table with the adjectives in the box.

| anxious embarrassed ~~excited~~ lonely pleased scared |

Positive feelings	**Negative feelings**
calm	angry
1 *excited*	2 _____
in a good mood	confused
3 _____	disappointed
	4 _____
	exhausted
	guilty
	5 _____
	nervous
	6 _____
	stressed

5 Complete the table below.

Adjective	**Adverb**
angry	1 *angrily*
2 _____	nicely
easy	3 _____
4 _____	fast
polite	5 _____

22 | Oxford 3000™

3.4 Speaking and writing

Speaking — telling and responding to a story

1a Complete the conversations with the words and phrases in the box.

> a funny thing happened   anyway   I was so angry
> it was all OK in the end   oh no   what happened
> ~~we had a bad experience~~   we were so pleased!
> you're joking

Conversation 1

A ¹ *We had a bad experience* when we were on holiday a few years ago. We hired a car and went exploring on the coast.
B Where were you?
A In the Canary Islands – in Fuerteventura, to be exact. So, ²_____, we were in this hired car and we decided to leave the main road. We were driving in some sand when, suddenly, the car got stuck.
B ³_____!
A That's what I thought. ⁴_____ with my husband – he went right when I said left, and suddenly, we were lost and stuck.
B So, what did you do?
A We walked about five kilometres to the nearest road, and then we got a taxi back to our hotel, where we called for help. ⁵_____, but it cost us €250 to get the car out of the sand!

Conversation 2

A ⁶_____ last weekend when we went for a walk. We parked our car in a pretty little village and walked over the mountains to the next village. We were hoping to get a bus back to our car.
B So, ⁷_____?
A We asked in a café about the buses, but there weren't any.
B ⁸_____!
A No, it's true. The café was full, so we left and started looking for a place to have lunch. We were walking along the road when a woman stopped her car and told us to get in.
B Why did she do that?
A She heard us ask about the buses in the café, so she knew where we wanted to go. You see, she was working in the village where our car was, and so she took us there on the way to work. ⁹_____!

b 3.3))) Listen and check.

Writing — email (1): describing an event

2 Choose the correct options to complete the email.

> Hi John,
>
> It was great to hear from you. Yes, thanks, I had a great time visiting my family. The best day was when we all went for a walk together. We started walking at midday and ¹(*a short time later*)/ *finally* / *while*, something really funny happened. We were walking along by the side of a river, ² *after a few minutes* / *then* / *when* my brother decided to try and jump across it. ³ *Suddenly* / *To begin with* / *While*, we saw him run towards the river, so we all stopped to watch him. Unfortunately, the river was wider than he thought and he landed right in the middle. ⁴ *At first* / *But after* / *Half an hour later*, we didn't say anything, ⁵ *at last* / *but then* / *next* my brother started laughing. That made the rest of us laugh, too. ⁶ *At first* / *When* / *In the end*, my sister went to help him get out of the river. As you can imagine, he was very wet!
>
> Anyway, I'll call you soon to see when I can show you the photos.
>
> Love, Jane

I can …	Very well	Quite well	More practice
understand and use adverbs of manner.	○	○	○
tell and respond to a story.	○	○	○
write an informal email describing an event.	○	○	○

23

4 Changes and challenges

4.1 Changing directions

Vocabulary life stages and events

1 Complete the sentences with the life stages in the box.

> about thirty-five   a child   elderly   in (her) early twenties
> in (her) late twenties   in (my) mid-twenties   in (her) sixties
> middle-aged   a teenager

1 I'm 25 on my next birthday. I'm _in my mid-twenties_.
2 My mum is 50. She's _____.
3 My sister is 21. She's _____.
4 My grandmother is 75. She's _____.
5 My sister-in-law is 28. She's _____.
6 My aunt is 63. She's _____.
7 My cousin is in her mid-thirties. She's _____.
8 My niece is eight. She's _____.
9 My other niece is fifteen. She's _____.

2 Match verbs 1–8 to phrases a–h to make life events.

1 change   a to swim
2 get   b time abroad
3 learn   c home
4 leave   d career
5 live   e a job
6 move   f house
7 pass   g with a partner
8 spend   h your driving test

3 Complete the phrases with the words in the box.

> have   go to   choose   get   leave   start

1 _start_ your own business
2 _____ your career
3 _____ university
4 _____ a baby
5 _____ married
6 _____ home

4 Complete the article about Bill Gates with the correct past simple form of the verbs in the box.

> decide   get   go   have   leave   retire   start   take up

BILL GATES: Success story

Born in 1955, Bill Gates
[1] _took up_ computing when he was at high school. But when he [2] _____ school, he [3] _____ to follow the same career as his father and he [4] _____ to university to study Law. Later, however, he changed to maths and computer science instead. In 1975, while he was still at university, he started writing computer software for a company called MITS. In 1977, he [5] _____ his own company, Microsoft, and ten years later, he became the youngest billionaire ever. The same year, he met his future wife, Melinda, and in 1994, they [6] _____ married. The couple [7] _____ their first child in 1996 and another two children in 1999 and 2002. Today, Bill Gates is one of the richest men in the world, although he [8] _____ from his normal job at Microsoft in 2008.

24 Oxford 3000™

Grammar verbs with -ing and to

5 Put the words in the right order to make questions.

1 learn did when drive you to
   When did you learn to drive?
2 did to you what wear decide
   _____
3 win you did to who want
   _____
4 to much you plan did spend how
   _____
5 would go like where to you
   _____
6 did stop why to you need
   _____

PRONUNCIATION weak form of *to*

6a 4.1))) Listen and check your answers to exercise **5**. Pay attention to the weak /tə/ pronunciation of *to*.

b 4.1))) Listen again. Pause the CD and repeat after each word.

7 Choose the correct option to complete the sentences.
1 I learned *to play* / *playing* the piano when I was a child.
2 Do you like *to live* / *living* in the country?
3 I hope *to retire* / *retiring* before I'm 65.
4 My brother stopped *to play* / *playing* basketball when he went to university.
5 I can't stand *to go* / *going* to the dentist's.
6 When did you decide *to move* / *moving* house?
7 My girlfriend enjoys *to do* / *doing* aerobics.
8 If it keeps *to rain* / *raining*, we'll go home.

➡ **STUDY TIP** Have one page for verbs with *-ing* and another page for verbs with *to* in your notebook. Make a note of new verbs as you come across them. This will make it easier for you to remember how to use the verbs.

8 Complete the article with the correct form of the verbs in the box.

| apply | ask | be | do | get up | go | leave | look for | think | ~~work~~ |

HOME | ABOUT | NEWS | BLOG

The **right** way to **change** your job

What can you do if you can't stand ¹ _working_ in the job that you're in and you'd like ² _____ something different? Below are some tips to help you if you're in this situation.

First of all, you need ³ _____ about what you like and don't like about your current job. This will help you decide the kind of job you want ⁴ _____ for.

If you decide ⁵ _____ a new job, spend some time updating your CV. Then send your new one to all your contacts. Learn ⁶ _____ patient, because changing your job can take a long time!

Even if you hate ⁷ _____ for work every morning, it's important to keep ⁸ _____ to the office until you have a new job.

When you get a job offer, plan ⁹ _____ your current job after you've had a holiday – imagine ¹⁰ _____ your new boss for two weeks off on your first day!

I can …

	Very well	Quite well	More practice
talk about life stages and events.	○	○	○
use verbs with *-ing* or *to*.	○	○	○

25

4.2 Living without the internet

Vocabulary internet activities

1 Replace the words in **bold** with the verbs and phrases in the box.

| blog   chat online   do research   ~~go online~~   log on   shop online |
| tweet   use social media |

1 Do you **use the internet** every day? _go online_
2 Do you ever **look for information** online? _____
3 Do any of your friends **regularly update their personal website**? _____
4 How often do you **talk to your friends on your computer or smartphone**? _____
5 Do you ever **post comments on the social networking site Twitter**? _____
6 Do you ever **buy things on the internet**? _____
7 Which is the first website you **connect** to every day? _____
8 How often do you **go on Facebook or Twitter**? _____

2a Match verbs in box A to words in box B to make phrases. Then complete the sentences with the phrases.

| A | deal   do   download   post   read   share   ~~text~~   update |
| B | ~~friends~~   music   online banking   personal information on a website   photos   the news   with emails   your Facebook page |

1 A What do you do when you're feeling lonely?
   B I _text friends_. They always make me feel better.
2 A What's the first thing you do on Monday mornings?
   B I _____. I usually have hundreds to answer.
3 A Do you ever buy a newspaper?
   B No, I _____ on the internet.
4 A Where do you pay your electricity bill?
   B On the internet. I _____ so I don't have to leave my house.
5 A How often do you use social media?
   B A lot. But you don't need to _____ every day – you can add photos and comments when you like.
6 A How did you listen to that song?
   B On my mobile phone. I often _____ from the internet.
7 A Have you got a digital camera?
   B No, I use my phone because it's easier to _____ with my friends.
8 A Are you worried about internet security?
   B Not really. I never _____.

b 4.2)) Now listen and check.

3 Complete the article with eight of the verbs in exercises **1** and **2a**.

The changing face of social media

If you ¹ _use_ social media, you'll know that Facebook and Twitter are two of the most popular sites. Users ² _____ online several times a day to ³ _____ to their account and check what's new. You can ⁴ _____ photos and ⁵ _____ videos on both sites but, in fact, they are quite different. Most people use Twitter to ⁶ _____ the news or follow celebrities who ⁷ _____ messages about what they're doing. Of course, it's easier to ⁸ _____ online on Facebook, because you can write as many words as you like. These sites are popular now, but the internet is always changing, so perhaps in the future we will use different ones.

4.1　**4.2**　4.3　4.4　4.5

Grammar *going to* and present continuous for the future

4 Write sentences with *going to* for photos 1–6.

1 _____ He's going to jump. _____
2 _____
3 _____
4 _____
5 _____
6 _____

5 Choose the more likely option, *be going to* or present continuous, to complete the conversations.

1 **A** Why are you turning the computer on?
   B Because I'm *checking /* (*going to check*) my emails.
2 **A** Your boyfriend's Facebook page still says he's single.
   B I know. He's *updating / going to update* it at the weekend.
3 **A** Would you like to have dinner with us on Sunday?
   B Sorry, we can't. My in-laws *are coming / are going to come* round.
4 **A** Where's your girlfriend going this evening?
   B She's *having / going to have* a coffee with a friend.
5 **A** Why did they tell us to sit down?
   B Because the plane *is landing / is going to land*.
6 **A** Let's go to the cinema tonight.
   B I can't. I'm *working / going to work* late.

6 Complete the conversation with the most suitable form of the verb in brackets, *be going to* or present continuous.

A It's your birthday soon, isn't it?
B Yes, it's on 11th March. ¹ *I'm going to be* (I/be) 40.
A 40! ² _____ (you/have) a party on the Big Day?
B No, I've got other plans. ³ _____ (I/take) a few days off with my wife.
A How exciting! Tell me all about it.
B ⁴ _____ (we/visit) Paris that weekend.
   ⁵ _____ (I/not work) on the Friday, so
   ⁶ _____ (we/fly) on Friday morning.
   Then ⁷ _____ (we/come) back on Sunday evening.
A What ⁸ _____ (you/do) in Paris?
B ⁹ _____ (we/go up) the Eiffel Tower, obviously. And ¹⁰ _____ (we/see) a show at the Moulin Rouge, too – I've already got the tickets.
A Well, I hope you have a great time.
B Thanks.

I can …	Very well	Quite well	More practice
talk about using the internet.	○	○	○
talk about plans and arrangements.	○	○	○

27

4.3 Vocabulary development

Vocabulary *get*

1 Complete the sentences with *get* and the words in the box.

| bored   cold   home   a job   ~~married~~   a phone call |
| some pizzas   some shoes |

1 They lived together for ten years before they decided to _get married_.
2 I've got a dress for my sister's wedding, but I need to _____.
3 How do you feel when you _____ in the middle of the night?
4 I go to work at 7.30 every morning, and I don't _____ until 8 p.m.
5 Is your brother going to university, or is he going to _____?
6 I don't feel like cooking. Can you _____ on the way home from work?
7 I _____ when I go on long journeys.
8 Winter starts next month, so it's going to _____.

2 Respond to the sentences with *get* and the words in the box.

| any presents   home earlier   a job   ~~a new one~~ |
| ready   a taxi |

1 A My car isn't working.
   B Why don't _you get a new one?_
2 A My partner hasn't got any money.
   B Why doesn't he _____
3 A We're going clubbing tonight.
   B Why don't you _____
4 A I had a horrible birthday.
   B Why didn't you _____
5 A It's late, and there aren't any buses.
   B Why don't we _____
6 A She never has time to have dinner.
   B Why doesn't she _____

Vocabulary review

3a Complete the phrases with the words in the box.

| ~~about~~   abroad   -aged   career   go to   have   in   married |
| partner   sixties |

1 _about_ thirty-five
2 in your _____
3 change _____
4 get _____
5 _____ your early twenties
6 _____ university
7 _____ a baby
8 middle _____
9 live with a _____
10 spend time _____

b Which are life stages and which are life events in exercise 3a?

4 Match verbs 1–11 to words and phrases a–k to form internet activities.

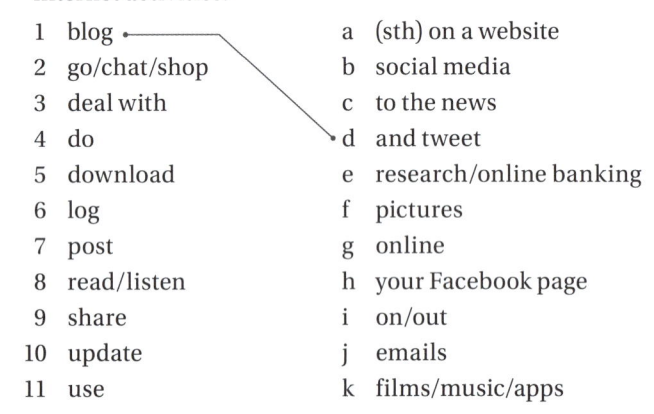

1 blog   a (sth) on a website
2 go/chat/shop   b social media
3 deal with   c to the news
4 do   d and tweet
5 download   e research/online banking
6 log   f pictures
7 post   g online
8 read/listen   h your Facebook page
9 share   i on/out
10 update   j emails
11 use   k films/music/apps

5 Complete the mind map with the verbs in the box to match the meaning of *get*.

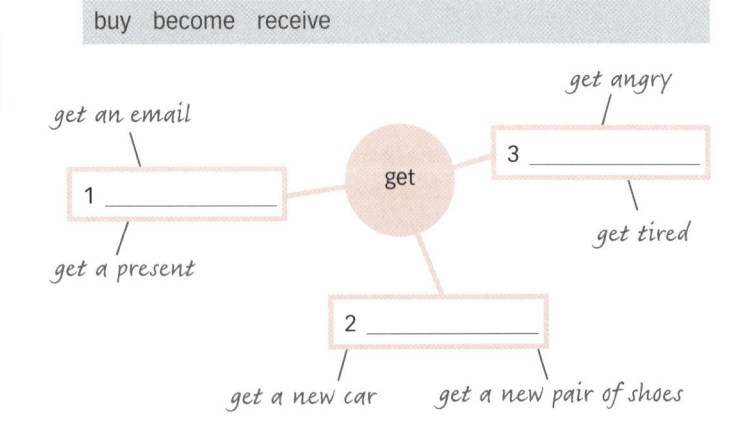

| buy   become   receive |

get an email
get a present
1 _____
get a new car   get a new pair of shoes
2 _____
get angry
3 _____
get tired

28   Oxford 3000™

4.4 Speaking and writing

Speaking inviting & making arrangements

1a Put the conversation in the correct order 1–8.

___ Sure. Is two o'clock OK for you?
___ I'm working on Saturday, but I'm free on Sunday.
___ Yeah, I'd love to.
_1_ Are you doing anything at the weekend?
___ Shall we meet outside the museum when it opens?
___ Two o'clock is perfect. See you there.
___ I'm afraid I can't go that early, because I'm playing tennis. Could we meet in the afternoon instead?
___ Do you fancy going to the Renoir exhibition at the Prado?

PRONUNCIATION inviting phrases

b 4.3))) Listen and check your answers.

c 4.3))) Listen again. Pause the CD and repeat after each word.

2 Complete the conversation with the phrases in the box.

| I'd like   ~~are you free~~   be great   how about   would you like |
| I can't make it   any good   sounds perfect   we could try |

A ¹ _Are you free_ next weekend?
B It depends. Why?
A It's my birthday on Friday and I'm having a party.
    ² _____ to come?
B I'm really sorry, but ³ _____ on Friday because I'm going to the theatre with some friends.
    ⁴ _____ having lunch together instead?
A That'd ⁵ _____!
B ⁶ _____ the new Japanese restaurant on the high street.
A Yes, ⁷ _____ that. Is one o'clock
    ⁸ _____ for you?
B ⁹ _____. See you on Friday.

Writing email (2): making arrangements

3 Look at the phrases below and choose the more informal ones. Then complete the email with the informal phrases.

- All the best / Love
- could we go out / how about going out
- Dear Suzanne /(Hi there)
- How are you doing? / I hope you are well
- I'd love to / We could
- I hope to hear from you soon / Speak soon
- I'm afraid / I'm really sorry but
- Is that OK for you? / Please let me know if that's OK

Sent: Friday 10.37

¹ _Hi there!_

² _____

³ _____ I can't make it to your birthday party. I'm going on a trip with my girlfriend that weekend so I won't be around.

Anyway, ⁴ _____ for a meal next week instead? Shall we meet for dinner on Friday evening? ⁵ _____ try the new Italian restaurant next to the cinema. ⁶ _____

Hope the party goes well.

⁷ _____

⁸ _____

Rob

I can ...	Very well	Quite well	More practice
understand and use *get*.	○	○	○
invite and make arrangements.	○	○	○
write an email to make arrangements.	○	○	○

4.5 Listening for pleasure

Ecological housing

1 Label the photo with the building materials in the box.

bricks ~~concrete~~ glass metal
plastic wood

2 (label 2) concrete

2 **4.4** Listen to a radio programme about a company that makes special houses.

3 **4.4** Listen again and complete the summary with the words and numbers in the box.

floor   parts   150   ~~printer~~   100   3,650   small   waste

> The WinSun Decoration Design Engineering Company makes special houses using a 3D [1] _printer_ . The machine is [2] _____ metres long and ten metres wide. It prints the houses in [3] _____ that people can put together later. The material for the houses is made from recycled industrial [4] _____ . The company is going to build [5] _____ new factories to do the recycling. The houses are quite [6] _____ and they only have one [7] _____ . They cost around [8] € _____ .

4 Think about the Chinese houses in the recording. Do you like the idea of houses like these? Why/Why not? Would they be popular in your country? Why/Why not?

Review: Units 3 and 4

Grammar

1 Choose the correct option to complete the sentences.
1. My sister enjoys (going) / to go to concerts.
2. I hope retiring / to retire before I'm 67.
3. We plan starting / to start our own business next year.
4. Can you imagine changing / to change your career?
5. My parents want moving / to move house.
6. They stopped playing / to play football when they left school.
7. Would you like coming / to come for dinner on Saturday evening?
8. My son keeps failing / to fail his exams.

2 Complete the conversation with the correct form of *be going to* and the words in brackets.

A What ¹ _are your parents going to do_ (your parents/do) when they retire?
B Well, first ² _____ (they/relax). But then, they have some plans. ³ _____ (they/not stay) at home all day.
A What ⁴ _____ (your dad/do)?
B ⁵ _____ (he/learn) Spanish. And ⁶ _____ (my mum/take up) a new hobby. She says she'd like to do yoga.

3 Complete the article with the past simple or past continuous form of the verbs in brackets.

Escape artist

Erik Weisz is better known as the escape artist Harry Houdini. He was born in Budapest, Hungary, but his family ¹ _moved_ (move) to the USA when he was only a child. He was 17 when his magic career began, but he ² _____ (not make) a lot of money at first. When he was 19, he met his wife while he ³ _____ (do) a show, and from then on the two ⁴ _____ (appear) together. The Houdinis ⁵ _____ (become) famous because of Harry's escape acts, which he did in front of a crowd. People usually felt very nervous while they ⁶ _____ (watch) him. Houdini always said that he ⁷ _____ (not feel) pain, so one day a student asked if he could test him. The man hit him in the stomach, but Houdini ⁸ _____ (lie) in bed at the time, so he wasn't in a good position. He died a few days later at the age of 52.

Vocabulary

4 Complete the sentences with a suitable word.
1. Her parents were very pl_eased_ when she and her boyfriend got engaged.
2. It was hot so we couldn't wait to d_____ into the swimming pool.
3. I felt l_____ when I first moved house.
4. Please don't dr_____ that mirror. It'll break.
5. He felt g_____ when he made his little sister cry.
6. I'll pick you up from the airport. What time do you l_____?

5 Complete the text with the verbs in the box.

| deal with   do   get   go   ~~leave~~   log on   retire   text |

Every year, the number of internet users rises. The most frequent users are teenagers between the ages of 16 and 18, but once they ¹ _leave_ school, these young adults don't ² _____ online as often. The internet is also popular with the elderly. Once people ³ _____, they have more time to ⁴ _____ to a computer and ⁵ _____ emails, for example. Teenagers use the internet on their mobile phones to ⁶ _____ friends on instant messaging services. Today more people ⁷ _____ online banking than before. People are also using the internet to try and ⁸ _____ a job.

Speaking

6 Complete the conversation with the phrases in the box.

| ~~are you free~~   do you fancy   how about   I'd love to
I had a bad experience   shall we   what happened
you're joking |

A Abigail, ¹ _are you free_ on Saturday night?
B Yes, I think so. Why?
A ² _____ going out for a meal?
B Yeah, ³ _____. Where are you thinking of going?
A ⁴ _____ trying that fish restaurant on the high street?
B Oh no! ⁵ _____ the last time I went there.
A Really? ⁶ _____?
B I was so ill the next day that I had to go to hospital.
A ⁷ _____! Well, ⁸ _____ go to an Indian restaurant instead?

31

5 Stuff and things

5.1 Your world in objects

Vocabulary adjectives for describing objects

1 Circle the word or phrase that is different.
 1 dark blue   metal   pale grey
 2 large   tiny   useful
 3 comfortable   heavy   light
 4 leather   plastic   thin
 5 gold   personal   ordinary
 6 antique   brand new   special

2 Match definitions 1–8 to words in the box.

| amazing gold leather light ordinary special useful valuable |

 1 made from an expensive metal   _gold_
 2 not weighing much   _____
 3 difficult to believe   _____
 4 made from the skin of animals   _____
 5 important for some reason   _____
 6 helpful and practical   _____
 7 costing a lot of money   _____
 8 very normal   _____

3 Complete the article with the words in the box.

| amazing antique brand new comfortable heavy large thin tiny |

Televisions: past and present

It's ¹ _amazing_ how much televisions have changed over the years. Early televisions were very ²_____ and they needed at least two people to carry them. It was difficult to see the image on an ³_____ television, because the screen was ⁴_____. Today, ⁵_____ televisions are a completely different shape. They are very ⁶_____, which makes them easier to carry, and they have a ⁷_____ screen, which is easy to see. And watching TV is much more ⁸_____ these days, because you don't have to get up from the sofa every time you want to change the channel!

PRONUNCIATION adjective word stress (2)

4a Underline the syllable we stress in the words. Which word has the stress on the second syllable?
 1 useful   5 special
 2 heavy   6 antique
 3 leather   7 plastic
 4 metal   8 tiny

b 5.1)) Listen and check.

c 5.1)) Listen again. Pause the CD and repeat after each word.

32 | Oxford 3000™

Grammar articles

5 Choose the correct option *a/an*, *the* or (✗) (= nothing) to complete the sentences.
1. It's my mother's birthday so I need to buy **a** / *the* / (✗) present.
2. Your coat is hanging in *a* / *the* / (✗) wardrobe.
3. I've forgotten *a* / *the* / (✗) name of that film we saw last night.
4. I've never liked *a* / *the* / (✗) big dogs, especially if they're barking.
5. Yesterday was *an* / *the* / (✗) ordinary day – we didn't do anything special.
6. *A* / *The* / (✗) ring my partner gave me is very valuable.
7. We never eat *a* / *the* / (✗) fast food because it isn't very healthy.
8. Our dishwasher is broken so we need to buy *a* / *the* / (✗) new one.

6 Read the article. Tick (✓) the correct articles and put a cross (✗) if the article is wrong. Correct the incorrect articles.
1. ✓
2. ✗   the planets
3. _____
4. _____
5. _____
6. _____
7. _____
8. _____
9. _____
10. _____
11. _____
12. _____

7 Complete the conversations with *a/an*, *the* or (✗) (= nothing).
1. A Where is *the* milk?
   B I put it back in _____ fridge.
2. A Do you want to have _____ shower?
   B Yes, please. Can I have _____ towel?
3. A Have you got _____ car?
   B Yes, but I prefer using _____ public transport.
4. A I've just read _____ great book. I cried at the end.
   B Really? I don't like _____ books with sad endings.
5. A Where can I find information about _____ cheap flights?
   B On _____ internet.
6. A Do your parents live in _____ house where you were born?
   B No, they moved to _____ countryside when they retired.

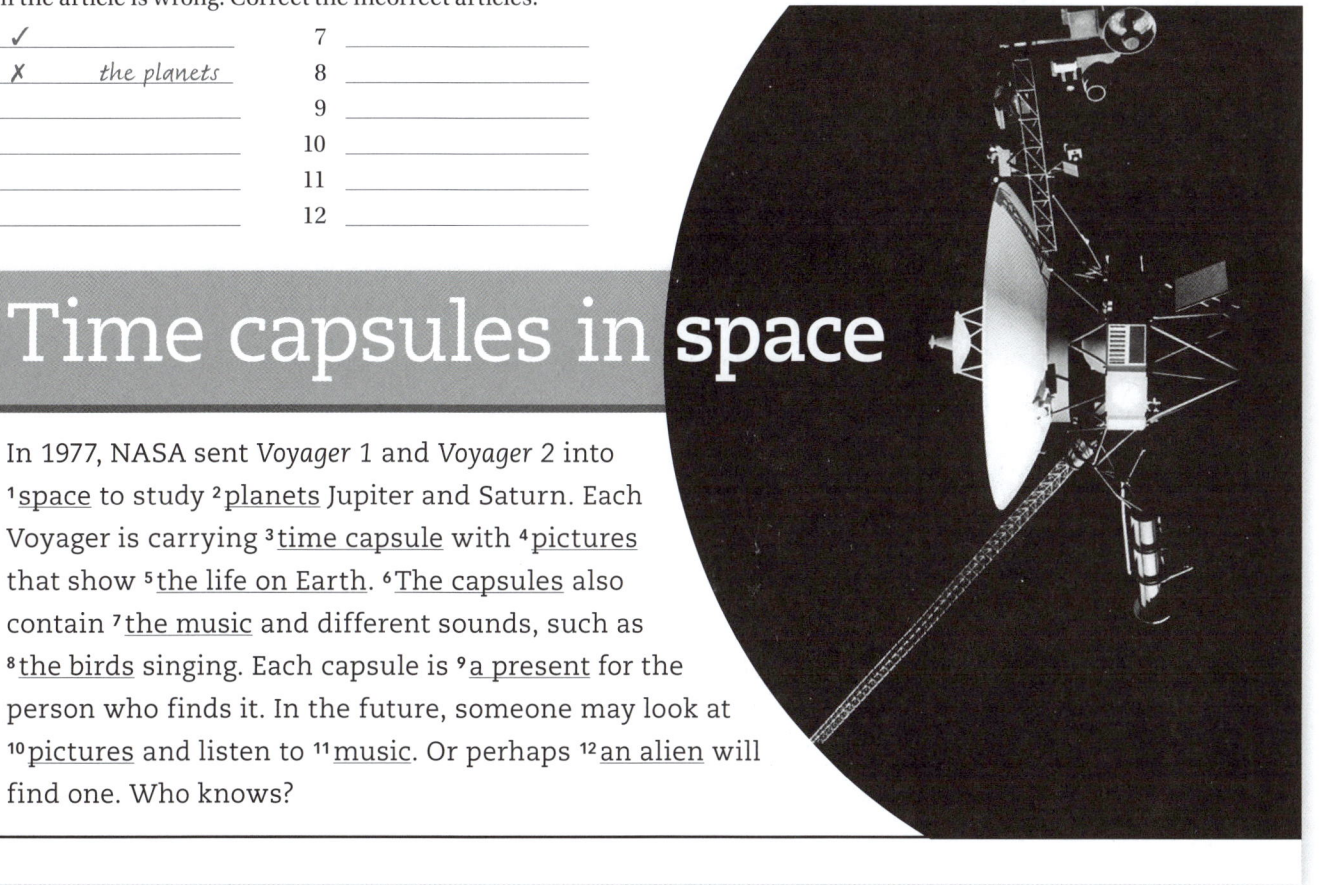

Time capsules in space

In 1977, NASA sent *Voyager 1* and *Voyager 2* into ¹space to study ²planets Jupiter and Saturn. Each Voyager is carrying ³time capsule with ⁴pictures that show ⁵the life on Earth. ⁶The capsules also contain ⁷the music and different sounds, such as ⁸the birds singing. Each capsule is ⁹a present for the person who finds it. In the future, someone may look at ¹⁰pictures and listen to ¹¹music. Or perhaps ¹²an alien will find one. Who knows?

I can …	Very well	Quite well	More practice
describe objects.	○	○	○
use articles.	○	○	○

5.2 It's all about the money

Vocabulary money

1a 5.2))) Listen and write six words connected to money.
   1 _bag_   _c_
   2 _____ ___
   3 _____ ___
   4 _____ ___
   5 _____ ___
   6 _____ ___

b 5.2))) Listen again and repeat the words.

c Match photos a–f to words 1–6 in exercise 1a.

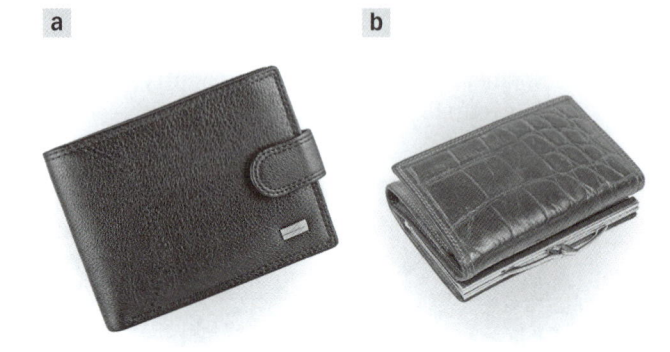

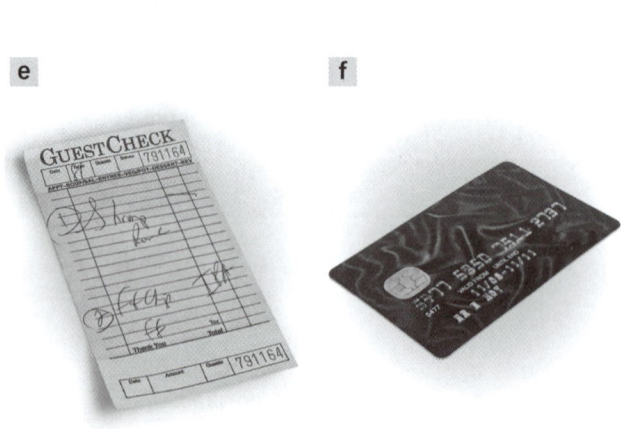

2 Complete the words in the sentences.
   1 Do you usually pay for your shopping in c_ash_ or by credit card?
   2 Do you have any ch_____ in your pocket right now?
   3 How old were you when you opened your first b_____ a_____?
   4 Have you ever been i_____ d_____ to a member of your family?
   5 Do you know the exact a_____ of money in your purse or wallet?
   6 Where do you check your b_____ – at the bank or on the internet?
   7 Do you own your house or flat or do you pay r_____?

3 Complete the text with the correct form of the verbs in the box.

| afford borrow lend ~~owe~~ pay for save up spend |

Borrowing from the bank

Most of us ¹ _owe_ money to a bank at some time in our lives because we can't ² _____ to buy a place to live without some help. Some people ³ _____ for the future when they are living with their parents, and others ⁴ _____ all their money on clothes and going out. But nearly everybody ⁵ _____ money from a bank to ⁶ _____ their first house. The problem is that when a bank ⁷ _____ you a lot of money, it can take many years to pay it back.

Grammar quantifiers

4 Choose the correct option to complete the sentences.
1 We took *any / some* great photos while we were on holiday.
2 My partner is very keen on reading. She's got *a lot of / too much* books.
3 There's too *much / many* sugar in my coffee. I can't drink it.
4 We live in a small village. There are only *a little / few* houses.
5 How *much / many* credit cards have you got?
6 The bill is right. There aren't *any / some* mistakes.
7 Do you do *many / much* exercise?
8 My brother has *enough / too many* money to buy a brand new car.

5 Complete the conversation with the quantifiers in the box.

a few   any   enough   lots of   many   much   ~~some~~
too much

A Great! We managed to find a parking space.
B Yes, but now we need ¹ _some_ money for the machine. Have you got ² _____ change?
A Yes, I think I've got ³ _____ coins in my purse, but not many. How ⁴ _____ money do we need?
B It depends how long we stay. Will 20 minutes give us ⁵ _____ time to speak to the manager?
A I'm not sure. There are usually ⁶ _____ people in the bank on Fridays and it can take a long time.
B OK, how about an hour?
A No, that's ⁷ _____ time. We don't have ⁸ _____ questions to ask. Let's put 40 minutes.
B Right. Come on, then. Let's go.

6 Complete the conversations with a quantifier from box A and a noun from box B.

A ~~a few~~   a little   any   enough   lots of   some
   too many   too much

B   biscuits   ~~days~~   food   friends   petrol   Portuguese
    shopping   things

1 A How long were you away?
  B Only _a few days_. Just for the weekend.
2 A Why did you call a taxi?
  B I had _____. I couldn't carry it all.
3 A Can you speak any foreign languages?
  B Yes, I speak English, Spanish and _____.
4 A Are you going camping alone?
  B No, we're going with _____. There will be six of us.
5 A Why aren't you hungry?
  B I've eaten _____. I finished the packet and I don't feel well!
6 A What's your hometown like?
  B Very interesting. There are _____ to see and do.
7 A What's the matter with the car?
  B We've stopped. We haven't got _____.
8 A Would you like a sandwich?
  B No, thanks. I've eaten _____ for one day.

I can …	Very well	Quite well	More practice
talk about money.	○	○	○
talk about quantity.	○	○	○

5.3 Vocabulary development

Vocabulary: suffixes

1 Complete the sentences with the correct form of the words in brackets.

1. My parents bought a new _digital_ camera for their holiday. (digit)
2. We haven't got any _____ for next weekend. (arrange)
3. I had a great time at the party. It was very _____. (enjoy)
4. Have you found a _____ for your house yet? (buy)
5. I never drive in the city centre. It's too _____. (stress)
6. It was a _____ day, the same as every other. (norm)
7. You have to pay extra to take sports _____ on a plane. (equip)
8. The match was a real _____. We lost 5-0. (disappoint)
9. We didn't sleep well because the beds weren't very _____. (comfort)
10. Can you give me some _____ about the exhibition, please? (inform)

2 Complete the text with the correct form of the words in brackets.

> If you have made the ¹ _decision_ (DECIDE) to throw away some of your ² _____ (POSSESS), then why not take them to a charity shop? These shops are ³ _____ (ESSENCE) for people in need, because your old things make money to help them. You can also find many ⁴ _____ (USE) things in the shops to buy. There are leather bags, children's toys and ⁵ _____ (BEAUTY) cards which you can send to friends and family on their birthdays. The clothes aren't usually very ⁶ _____ (FASHION), but you can sometimes find something ⁷ _____ (SUIT) for a special occasion. In some of the shops you can even find ⁸ _____ (COMPUTE)!

➡ **STUDY TIP** Some words are easier to remember than others. Write an example sentence for the words that you find particularly difficult and try to memorize the sentence. This will help you remember difficult words.

Vocabulary review

3 Complete the table with the headings in the box.

age colour material opinion size / shape weight

¹ _colour_	dark blue pale grey
² _____	amazing comfortable ordinary personal special useful
³ _____	heavy light
⁴ _____	gold leather metal plastic
⁵ _____	antique brand new
⁶ _____	large thin tiny

4 Complete the table with the words in the box.

afford balance cash lend note pay for rent save up

Money: nouns
amount   bag   ¹ _balance_   bank account   bill
² _____   change   coin   credit card   ³ _____
purse   receipt   ⁴ _____   ticket   wallet

Money: verbs
⁵ _____   borrow   ⁶ _____   owe
⁷ _____   ⁸ _____   spend ... on

5 Complete the table with the correct form of the words in the box.

buy disappoint inform norm suit use

Noun suffixes

-ment: arrangement,   ¹ _disappointment_,   equipment

-ion: condition,   ² _____,   possession

-er: ³ _____,   computer,   scooter

Adjective suffixes

-ful: beautiful,   stressful,   ⁴ _____

-able: comfortable,   enjoyable,   fashionable,   ⁵ _____

-al: digital,   essential,   ⁶ _____

5.4 Speaking and writing

Speaking explaining words you don't know

1a Put the conversation in the correct order 1–9.

___ That's right. Do you know what I mean?
___ Well, can you describe it for me?
___ Oh, hello. Yes, I am, but I don't know the word in English.
___ Yes, it's a thing that you use to keep warm in the winter.
_1_ Good morning. Are you looking for anything in particular?
___ No, it looks like a carpet, but it's smaller.
___ Yes, I do. It's a rug. Come with me and I'll show you where they are.
___ Is it something you wear?
___ And do you put it on the floor?

b 5.3))) Listen and check.

2 Complete the conversation with the phrases in the box.

> Exactly! That's what I'm looking for.   what's it called?
> You use it to dry yourself   I've forgotten the word in English.
> It's quite big, like a sheet.

A Hi. Can I help you?
B Yes, I'm looking for … ¹ _what's it called?_
A Yes?
B ² _____ .
A Well, what does it look like?
B ³ _____ .
A Do you mean a duvet?
B No, no. ⁴ _____ after you have a shower.
A Oh! You mean a towel!
B ⁵ _____ .
A Good. The towels are over there on the right.
B Thank you very much.
A You're welcome.

Writing email (3): returning an online product

3 Complete the email with the phrases in the box.

> Could you please send   get a refund   I didn't receive
> I'm afraid I'm not happy   I'd like to return   Yours sincerely
> recently ordered   they are completely different

Dear Sir/Madam,

Re: order number 492JM

¹ I _recently ordered_ some headphones from your online store. I received them this morning, but ² _____ with them because they're damaged. Also, ³ _____ from the headphones in the photo on the website. Those were purple and they came with a purple bag. ⁴ _____ the bag.

As a result, ⁵ _____ the headphones.

⁶ _____ me the headphones that are in the photo on the website? If this is not possible, I would like to ⁷ _____ .

⁸ _____

Yasmin Husseini

I can …	Very well	Quite well	More practice
understand and use suffixes.	○	○	○
explain words I don't know.	○	○	○
write an email to return an online product.	○	○	○

37

6 People

6.1 The quiet revolution

Vocabulary adjectives for describing character

1 Complete the puzzle to discover the hidden adjective.

```
1 S O C I A B L E
2
3
    4
  5
 6
    7
   8
```

1 not shy about speaking with people
2 very intelligent
3 not talking much
4 not wanting to work
5 not putting things in the right place
6 very sure about what you are doing
7 not stupid
8 not telling lies

2 Choose the correct option to complete the sentences.
1 You're really *clever* / *sociable*. You always get good marks in exams.
2 My sister gets nervous when she meets new people. She's quite *shy* / *tidy*.
3 I don't usually mind waiting. I'm quite *patient* / *confident*.
4 We're a bit *lazy* / *unsociable*. We prefer to be on our own.
5 Most people think my brother is *untidy* / *stupid*, but actually, he's really smart.
6 My partner enjoys her job and does it well. She's very *hard-working* / *honest*.
7 My husband likes having things in the right place. He's very *tidy* / *smart*.
8 Most of my friends are artists. They are all very *creative* / *quiet*.

PRONUNCIATION adjective word stress (3)

3a Underline the syllables which are stressed in the words in the box. Then complete the table.

clever confident creative honest lazy patient sociable untidy

Oo	Ooo	oOo
clever		

b 6.1))) Listen and check.

c 6.1))) Listen again. Pause the CD and repeat after each word.

38 | Oxford 3000™

Grammar making comparisons

4 Complete the table with the comparative and superlative forms of the adjectives.

Adjective	Comparative adjective	Superlative adjective
1 bad	_worse_	the _____
2 good	_____	the _____
3 honest	_____	the _____
	less honest	the least honest
4 lazy	_____	the _____
5 old	_____	the _____
6 smart	_____	the _____
7 sociable	_____	the _____
	less sociable	the least sociable
8 tidy	_____	the _____

5 Write sentences using comparative or superlative adjectives.
1 fruit / healthy / chocolate
   Fruit is healthier than chocolate.
2 rugs / small / carpets
   _____
3 Monday / bad / day of the week
   _____
4 gold / expensive / plastic
   _____
5 I think / skiing / exciting / sport
   _____
6 they say flying / safe / way to travel
   _____
7 your English / good / mine
   _____
8 my hometown / lively / place I know
   _____

6 Rewrite the comparative sentences with (*not*) *as … as*. Use the adjectives in the box.

big dangerous dark ~~difficult~~ hard-working old thin wet

1 English is easier than Chinese.
  English _isn't as difficult as Chinese._
2 Today is drier than yesterday.
  Today _____
3 A duvet is thicker than a sheet.
  A duvet _____
4 My brother is lazier than me.
  He _____
5 Your hair is lighter than mine.
  Your hair _____
6 I'm younger than my wife.
  I'm _____
7 My office is smaller than yours.
  My office _____
8 Cars are safer than motorbikes.
  Cars _____

I can …	Very well	Quite well	More practice
describe character.	○	○	○
talk about similarities and differences.	○	○	○

39

6.2 A long way home

Vocabulary family

1 Complete the table with the correct family words.

Females	Males
aunt	1 _uncle_
2 _____	cousin
daughter	3 _____
4 _____	grandfather
great-grandmother	5 _____
6 _____	half-brother
mother-in-law	7 _____
8 _____	nephew
stepmother	9 _____

2 Complete the words in the conversations.
1 A Is that your boyfriend?
   B Yes, his name's Rashid. We're a c_ouple_.
2 A Have you got any brothers or sisters?
   B No, I haven't. I'm an o_____ ch_____.
3 A Have you got a large family?
   B Yes, but I only see my r_____ at weddings.
4 A Has your friend left her husband?
   B Yes. They're going to g_____ d_____.
5 A You look exactly like your sister.
   B Yes, we're tw_____.
6 A Are you married?
   B No, I'm a s_____ p_____.
7 A How many children would you like?
   B Two or three. But I'd also like to a_____ one.
8 A Is your sister going out with Matt?
   B Yes. They're going to g_____ e_____ next month.

3 Complete the article with the words in the box.

couples   daughters   get divorced   grandfathers
only child   relatives   ~~single parent~~   uncles

Family facts around the world

Did you know ...?

- Children have a mother and a father who are their parents. However, more children live with a [1] _single parent_ in the Americas, Europe, Oceania and Africa than in the rest of the world. In these families, it is the oldest relatives, such as grandmothers and [2] _____, who help to look after the younger children.

- Children usually live with their parents and their brothers and sisters. Sharing a house with other [3] _____ is more common in Asia, the Middle East, South America and Africa. People in these areas often live with grandparents and great-grandparents, but some live with aunts and [4] _____, too.

- The main reason for finding a partner is usually to form a new family together. [5] _____ are more likely to be married in Africa, Asia and the Middle East. In the Americas, Europe and Oceania more people [6] _____ than in other places.

- Families in some countries have more children than families in others. It is unusual for African families to have an [7] _____. In Nigeria, women usually have five or six sons and [8] _____.

4a Circle the word with a different vowel sound.
1 son   mother   (adopt)
2 aunt   father   parent
3 divorced cousin   uncle
4 daughter engaged   sister-in-law
5 couple   husband   only

PRONUNCIATION family words

b 6.2))) Listen and check.

c 6.2))) Listen again. Pause the CD and repeat after each word.

40 Oxford 3000™

Grammar: present perfect simple and past simple

→ **STUDY TIP** The list of irregular verbs on p.166 of your Coursebook contains the past participle of these verbs, as well as the past simple forms. The past participle is in the third column of the list, and we use it to form the present perfect simple. As you did with the past simple forms, study five verbs every day until you remember the past participle forms of each verb on the list. This will make it easier for you to use the present perfect simple correctly.

5 Use the words to write present perfect simple sentences and questions.

1 my grandfather / give me / his old car
   My grandfather has given me his old car.

2 they / not hear / from their son this week
   _____

3 your friend / ever / speak / to her stepbrother?
   _____

4 I / never / meet / my cousins in Australia
   _____

5 my sister / find / a new boyfriend
   _____

6 we / not see / our great-grandparents recently
   _____

7 my mother-in-law / never / invite us / for a meal
   _____

8 you / ever / fall / down the stairs?
   _____

6 Choose the correct option to complete the sentences.

1 Have you ever lent money to your family?
   No, but I *'ve lent / (lent)* some to a friend last week.
2 Have you ever been camping?
   Yes, but we *haven't enjoyed / didn't enjoy* it last time.
3 Have you been on a plane?
   No, I *haven't flown / didn't fly* before.
4 Have you ever seen the Eiffel Tower?
   Yes, I *'ve lived / lived* in Paris when I was young.
5 Have you ever done yoga?
   Yes, I *'ve had / had* a yoga class yesterday.
6 Have you ever driven on the motorway?
   Yes, I *'ve done / did* it lots of times.
7 Have you ever been to China?
   No, but I *'ve been / went* to Japan a few years ago.

7 Complete the conversation with the correct present perfect simple or past simple form of the verb in brackets.

A ¹ *Have you ever done* (you/ever/do) anything really exciting?
B Well, ² _____ (I/not/travel) into space, if that's what you mean! But, yes, ³ _____ (I/drive) a Ferrari.
A Really? When ⁴ _____ (you/do) that?
B Last year. ⁵ _____ (my girlfriend/give) me 30 minutes in a Ferrari as a present.
A How far ⁶ _____ (you/go)?
B ⁷ _____ (I/not/drive) very far – about 50 km.
A ⁸ _____ (you/enjoy) it?
B Yes, it was fun.
A What about your girlfriend? ⁹ _____ (she/ever/do) anything similar?
B Yes, she loves exciting sports and she often goes skiing and surfing. ¹⁰ _____ (she/climb) Everest too, and ¹¹ _____ (she/fly) a helicopter. But ¹² _____ (she/not/jump) out of a plane. I'm going to give her a parachute jump for her next birthday!

I can ...	Very well	Quite well	More practice
talk about family.	○	○	○
talk about experiences.	○	○	○

6.3 Vocabulary development

Vocabulary adjective prefixes

1 Complete the table with the opposite of the adjectives in the box.

| fair friendly happy healthy honest kind lucky necessary organized patient pleasant polite possible usual |

dis-	un-	im-
	unfair	

2 Complete the conversations with eight words from exercise 1.

1 A Does anyone in your family wear strange clothes?
   B Yes, I've got an aunt who wears _unusual_ hats.
2 A Did you find the homework difficult?
   B I couldn't do it. It was _____.
3 A What do you do to keep fit?
   B Nothing. I'm really _____ at the moment.
4 A Does your niece tell lies?
   B Yes, she's a bit _____.
5 A Why are those children rude?
   B They're always _____.
6 A What's that horrible smell?
   B I don't know, but it's very _____.
7 A Is your husband tidy?
   B No, he's a bit _____.
8 A Why is your brother sad?
   B He's _____ because he's getting divorced.

Vocabulary review

3 Complete the table with the opposite adjectives for describing character.

| confident lazy sociable stupid untidy |

Adjective	Opposite
clever/smart	1 _stupid_
2 _____	shy
hard-working	3 _____
quiet	
4 _____	unsociable
tidy	5 _____

4 Complete the family words.

1 c o u s i n
2 gr _ _ t-gr _ ndm _ th _ r
3 h _ lf-s _ st _ r
4 n _ ph _ w
5 c _ _ pl _
6 g _ t _ ng _ g _ d
7 r _ l _ t _ v _ s
8 tw _ ns

5 Complete the table with the opposite form of the adjectives in the box.

| friendly healthy lucky organized pleasant polite |

dis-	dishonest, 1 _disorganized_
im-	impatient, 2 _____, impossible
un-	unfair, 3 _____, unhappy
	4 _____, unkind
	5 _____, unnecessary
	6 _____, unusual

42 Oxford 3000™

6.4 Speaking and writing

Writing responding to news on social media

1 Circle the incorrect response.
   1 **Tony**   Holiday cancelled. Not happy!
     Kristine Bad luck! / *I'm SO jealous!* / Sorry to hear that.
   2 **Marta**   Just arrived at the airport. Barbados here we come!
     Sarah   You lucky thing! / Have a fab time! / Get well soon.
   3 **Mary**   Great news – won my tennis match!
     John   Congratulations! / Thinking of you. / Well done!
   4 **Jill**   Bad back – can't move!
     Stuart   Get well soon. / Good luck! / Hope you feel better soon.
   5 **Doris**   My new niece – isn't she beautiful!
     Dominique You'll be fine. / Great pic. / Love the pic!
   6 **Eldon**   Driving test tomorrow …
     Ania   Best of luck! / Fingers crossed! / Well done!

2 Complete the sentences with *just*, *already* or *yet*.
   1 He's _____ left the office – if you run, you might see him in the car park.
   2 They've _____ booked their flights to Goa in September, so you don't need to do it for them.
   3 Have you seen the new Scarlet Johansson film _____?
   4 He's _____ seen his exam results online, he doesn't need to go to the school.

Speaking giving and responding to news

3 Choose the correct options to complete the conversations.
   Conversation 1
   A Hey, Becky. ¹*Guess what?* / Never mind.
   B What?
   A I'm getting engaged!
   B Congratulations! ²*That's great news!* / What a pity!
   A We're having a party on May 1st. Can you come?
   B Yes, I'd love to. ³*Oh dear. I'm sorry* / *I'm really happy for you*.
   Conversation 2
   A Hiya. Are you OK?
   B No, not really. My grandfather's in hospital.
   A ⁴*Oh no!* / *Oh wow!* What's the problem?
   B He fell over last night.
   A ⁵*Oh dear. I'm sorry.* / *How amazing!*
   B He spent all night on the floor of the bathroom.
   A ⁶*That's wonderful!* / *What a shame!* What have the doctors said?
   B I don't know yet. I'm going to visit him this evening.
   A ⁷*Never mind.* / *Guess what?* I'm sure he'll be OK.

4 Read the lines from two conversations. Decide if they belong to Conversation 1 or Conversation 2. Write *1* or *2*.
   _1_ A Have you heard the news? About my sister and her husband?
   _2_ A I've got some bad news for you, Danny.
   ___ B What?
   ___ B No. What?
   ___ A Tom and Alice are getting divorced.
   ___ A They're adopting a baby.
   ___ B That's terrible! What happened?
   ___ B How exciting! When are they getting him?
   ___ A They're going to get him next month.
   ___ A Tom moved out last week.
   ___ B Oh wow! I can't wait to see him!
   ___ B How awful! I'll call Alice tonight.

I can …	Very well	Quite well	More practice
understand and use adjective prefixes.	○	○	○
give and respond to news.	○	○	○
use the present perfect simple with *just*, *already* and *yet*.	○	○	○

43

6.5 Reading for pleasure

Little Rock

1 Look at the photo. What kind of discrimination does it show? Circle the correct answer 1, 2, 3 or 4.

1 age
2 racial
3 religious
4 sex

2 Read an extract from the biography of Martin Luther King.

3 Choose the correct options to complete the extract summary.

> There were problems in the South because the local population wanted the schools to be **1** mixed / (segregated). Change started to come in the 1950s when the law changed **2** *and black children wanted to go to Central High School / and white children wanted to go to another school*. On 2nd September Orval Faubus tried to **3** *break the law / enforce the law*. Later in the same month **4** *there were more protests outside Central High / everything calmed down*. The president **5** *reacted to the situation / ignored the situation*. From then on the black children were protected **6** *by soldiers / by police*.

4 Think about the racism in the story. Can you think of other countries in the world where racism has been an important issue? Do people worry about racism in your country? Why/Why not?

The story so far
Martin Luther King Junior (January 15th, 1929 – April 4th, 1968) was the leader of the African-American Civil Rights Movement. The incident in the extract took place just after he and his new wife moved back to the South of the United States.

Big trouble in Little Rock

There were many other things in the South that needed to change. Schools were segregated: white children went to all-white schools, black children went to all-black schools. Although there were more black children than white children in the South, much more money was spent on white schools than on black schools.

But in 1954 the law was changed. Now it was against the law to have different schools for black children and white children. The new law said that all schools had to take both black children and white children.

Change came slowly to the South. Many white people hated the new law, and in many Southern states, they refused to obey it. Arkansas was one of these states. In the state capital, Little Rock, nine black students tried to enter the Central High School at the start of the 1957–58 school year. Little Rock soon became one of the most famous places in the story of the fight for civil rights.

On 2 September, the night before the start of the new school year, the leader of the Arkansas government, Orval Faubus, ordered the National Guard to stand outside Central High School. He told them to stop any black student from entering the school, because he was afraid of trouble from protesters. The school was closed. But a judge said that Faubus could not use the National Guard to do something that was against the law. On 23 September the Little Rock police took the nine black students into Central High. A crowd of more than a thousand white people tried to stop the black students from entering. The crowd rioted and attacked the police. The pictures of the riot were seen all over the world, and many Americans were shocked to see such ugly attacks in their own country. Next day, the President of the United States, Dwight D. Eisenhower, ordered the army to Little Rock. A thousand soldiers entered Little Rock Central High School. Every morning the nine black children walked to the school, and every morning the soldiers protected them as they walked through crowds of angry whites.

Text extract from *Oxford Bookworms Readers: Little Rock*

Review: Units 5 and 6

Grammar

1 Choose the correct option to complete the sentences.
1. Alaska is the *larger /(largest)/ most large / least large* state in the USA.
2. There weren't *any / little / much / some* black US presidents before Barack Obama.
3. We *go / has been / have been / went* to Disneyland last year.
4. You'll need *any / some / much / a little* American dollars if you're going to the US.
5. The United States was *a / an / - / the* country with problems in the 1950s and 1960s.
6. *Are / Did / Do / Have* you ever been to San Francisco?
7. New York is *more / most / as / less* important than Little Rock.

2 Complete the text. Write one word in each space.

Mahatma Gandhi is one of the ¹ *most* famous human rights leaders who has ever lived. There are few people who ² _____ never heard of him. Gandhi was born in India in 1869, but after university he went to London to become ³ _____ lawyer. From there he went to South Africa, where he tried to help ⁴ _____ Indian immigrants who lived there. During his twenty years in South Africa, he went to prison ⁵ _____ times, but in the end conditions got better. Gandhi returned home in 1915, but the situation in India was almost as bad ⁶ _____ in South Africa because India had a British government. Gandhi protested against the British, but he was never violent. Soon ⁷ _____ of people were following him. The British left India in 1947, but Gandhi was assassinated the following year. Since then, his birthday has ⁸ _____ a national holiday in India.

Vocabulary

3 Circle the word that is different.
1. metal   (cash)   leather   plastic
2. lend   owe   adopt   borrow
3. antique   confident   lazy   sociable
4. only child   bank account   half-sister   single
5. engaged   special   useful   valuable
6. balance   change   uncle   rent
7. smart   tidy   creative   divorced

4 Complete the text with the words in the box.

| amount   comfortable   couple   ~~ordinary~~   patient |
| quiet   son |

Aung San Suu Kyi is no ¹ *ordinary* woman. Because of her ideas, she spent more than twenty years of her life under house arrest at her home in Myanmar. Towards the end, her house was not very ² _____ because she had no electricity. But Ms Suu Kyi was ³ _____ and today she is free. She was born in Myanmar in 1945, but she went to university in Oxford, England, where she met her husband. The ⁴ _____ got married in 1972 and had their first ⁵ _____ in 1973. Ms Suu Kyi returned to Myanmar in 1988 to look after her mother, who was ill, and she stayed to protest against the government. The country's leaders put her under house arrest because they wanted her to be ⁶ _____. In 1991, Ms Suu Kyi received the Nobel Peace Prize for her work, which came with a large ⁷ _____ of money.

5 Complete the sentences with the correct form of the words in brackets.
1. The staff in that shop are very *unfriendly*. (friendly)
2. Moving house can be very _____. (stress)
3. That was very _____ of you to take that money without asking. (honest)
4. Is this film _____ for children to watch? (suit)
5. The party was a _____ – nobody enjoyed it. (disappoint)
6. I keep all my most valuable _____ on my chest of drawers. (possess)

Speaking

6 Put the words in the correct order to make sentences.
1. forgotten / English / the / in / I've / word
   I've forgotten the word in English.
2. really / you / happy / I'm / for
   _____
3. you / news / heard / Have / the
   _____
4. what / for / I'm / That's / looking
   _____
5. open / use / doors / it / You / to
   _____

45

7 Travel

7.1 On the move

Vocabulary transport

1 Match the two halves of the sentences.
 1 It's safer to cross the main — c road at the lights.
 2 I can only use my bus — d pass to travel in the city centre.
 3 Do you go to work by public — e transport or by car?
 4 We bought our tickets in — a advance so they were less expensive.
 5 I got caught in a huge traffic — b jam on the way to work.

2 Replace the words in **bold** with the words in the box.

convenient crowded fare fuel ~~greener~~ pollution reliable

 1 Riding a bike is **better for the environment** than going by car. _greener_
 2 The **dirty air** in the city centre is quite bad this morning. _____
 3 The station was **full of people** because the train was late. _____
 4 What **petrol or diesel** does your car use? _____
 5 The bus service in my town isn't very **regular and efficient**. _____
 6 If you live near a station, the metro is very **easy and quick to use**. _____
 7 How much is the **money you pay to travel** from Paris to London by train? _____

3 Complete the article with the words in the box.

convenient crowded fare greener main roads
public transport reliable ~~traffic jams~~

Getting around in Moscow

Moscow is one of the worst cities in the world for driving and drivers sit for more than twenty days a year in [1] _traffic jams_ in the Russian capital. The [2] _____ of the city centre are busiest during the early morning rush hour, which lasts from 8 a.m. to 11 a.m., so many residents leave their cars at home and use [3] _____ instead. The Moscow metro is the most [4] _____ way to get around the city because it is quick, cheap and easy to use. Metro entrances are marked with a large red letter 'M' and the [5] _____ is cheaper if you buy a ticket for ten or twenty rides. Some of the stations are beautiful, such as Mayakovskaya Station, to the north of the green line. The trains are generally [6] _____ and passengers hardly ever have to wait for more than three minutes. However, up to nine million people a day use the metro so it can get very [7] _____ when people are travelling to and from work. There are also buses in Moscow, but the metro is much faster – and [8] _____ – than the bus.

Grammar prediction (*will, might*)

4 Complete the conversations with the contraction of *will* + the verbs in the box.

~~be~~ have park pass rain win

1 **A** Will you be home for dinner?
   B No, I _'ll be_ late.
2 **A** My wife is taking her driving test today.
   B I'm sure she _____.
3 **A** We're going to a party tonight.
   B I know you _____ a good time.
4 **A** What will we do if we can't find a parking space?
   B We _____ in the car park.
5 **A** Why have you got an umbrella?
   B Because I think it _____.
6 **A** Is your team good?
   B Yes, but I don't think they _____.

PRONUNCIATION *might*

5a 7.1))) Listen to two sentences with *might*. Notice that when *might* is stressed, you sound less sure.
    I might buy a car. (= quite sure)
    I <u>might</u> buy a car. (= not very sure)

b 7.1))) Listen again. Pause the CD and repeat after each sentence.

c 7.2))) Listen to five more sentences and decide if they are 'quite sure' or 'not very sure'.
    1 _quite sure_
    2 _____
    3 _____
    4 _____
    5 _____

6 Choose the correct option to complete the sentences.
  1 I told him it's my birthday next week, but I know he *might* / *'ll* forget.
  2 Let's take a map. We *might* / *'ll* get lost.
  3 I'm not sure about that film. You *might not* / *won't* like it.
  4 The flight is too expensive. I probably *might not* / *won't* have enough money.
  5 We're not sure how we're getting home. We *might* / *'ll* take a taxi.
  6 We invited my grandparents to the party, but I don't think they *might* / *'ll* come.
  7 It's very late. We probably *might not* / *won't* arrive on time.
  8 I don't know what to do tonight. I *might not* / *won't* go out.

7 Complete the text with *will* or *might* and the verbs in brackets.

▶ Mars One

Mars One is an amazing project that is sending a group of people to live on the planet Mars. The first four astronauts ¹ _will leave_ (leave) Earth in April 2024 to start the 210-day journey to the Red Planet. They ² _____ (not see) their family and friends again because the trip is only one way. Everybody knows that the journey ³ _____ (be) dangerous and the astronauts ⁴ _____ (not arrive) on Mars safely. Let's hope they are lucky and they land without any problems. Living on Mars will be very different from living on Earth because they ⁵ _____ (spend) all of their time inside. They ⁶ _____ (not meet) any different people for the next two years, so it's possible they ⁷ _____ (feel) bored. However, a second group of astronauts ⁸ _____ (join) the first group in 2026 so they will have more people to talk to. Mars One is planning to make a reality show about the project, and the organizers are sure that everybody on Earth ⁹ _____ (watch) the astronauts land on Mars. It ¹⁰ _____ (be) interesting to see what they think about their new home and their new lives.

I can …	Very well	Quite well	More practice
talk about transport.	○	○	○
make predictions.	○	○	○

47

7.2 Getting away

Vocabulary holidays

1 Match definitions 1–8 to words in the box.

accommodation culture ~~flight~~ guidebook insurance research reviews souvenir

1 a journey by air _flight_
2 a place to live or stay _____
3 a thing that you buy to remind you of your holiday _____
4 an agreement with a company that will pay your costs if you have an accident, etc. _____
5 pages full of information for tourists _____
6 the study of something to find out more information _____
7 the customs and ideas of a country _____
8 opinions about hotels and restaurants, etc. _____

2 Complete the phrases with the correct verbs in the box.

~~buy~~ experience explore get go lie read try

What can you do …
1 in a shop the day before you go home?
   buy souvenirs
2 on a nice day in a hotel? _____ by the pool
3 in a bank before you travel? _____ foreign currency
4 in a restaurant or at a street stall? _____ the local food
5 in the airport or on the plane? _____ a guidebook
6 in a very beautiful city? _____ sightseeing
7 at a market or a festival? _____ the local culture
8 in a car you hire for a few days? _____ the area

3 Match words from A to words from B to make verb phrases. Then complete the article with the verb phrases.

A apply ~~book~~ buy choose hire read

B a car for a visa online reviews travel insurance your accommodation ~~your flight~~

Online holidays

Technology has changed the way we do everything, especially when it comes to organizing a summer holiday. You no longer need to go to a travel agency because you can do everything yourself on the internet. Many airlines have websites where you can ¹ _book your flight_ and these companies usually offer extra services, too. If you are worried about losing your possessions, you can often ² _____ from the company you fly with. If the place you are staying in is far from the airport, you might want to ³ _____ to get there. When you have got your flight, you need to ⁴ _____. The best way to do this is to ⁵ _____ for each of the hotels you are interested in. These will give you an idea of the location and quality of the hotel. The internet will also tell you if you need anything special for your trip, like a visa. While it might not be possible to ⁶ _____ online, there are websites that will tell you which documents you need and where to go to get one. The internet has made it much easier to organize a holiday and it has also made it a lot cheaper.

PRONUNCIATION stress in phrases

4a Underline the unstressed syllables in the phrases.
1 book your flight   5 read a guidebook
2 lie by the pool   6 apply for a visa
3 try the local food   7 go sightseeing
4 hire a car   8 explore the area

b 7.3)) Listen and check.

c 7.3)) Listen again. Pause the CD and repeat after each word.

48 Oxford 3000™

Grammar *something, anyone, everybody, nowhere, etc.*

5 Complete definitions 1–8 with *something, anyone, everybody, nowhere,* etc for the words in **bold**. In some cases there are two possible answers.
1 It's _somewhere_ you go to relax in the summer. **pool**
2 It's how you feel when you've learned _____ quickly. **clever**
3 It's a thing you use on public transport to go _____ more cheaply. **bus pass**
4 It's an adjective for a seat where _____ wants to sit. **comfortable**
5 It's a thing you use when _____ is clean. **cloth**
6 It's an adjective for a person who doesn't say _____. **quiet**
7 It's how you feel when you haven't got _____ to talk to. **lonely**
8 It's an adjective to describe a place where _____ can move because there are too many people. **crowded**

6 Choose the correct options to complete the text.

Beautiful Krakow

If you're looking for ¹*anywhere / everywhere / somewhere* interesting to go for your next holiday, why not try Krakow in Poland? The city is more than 750 years old, and ²*anywhere / nowhere / somewhere* in Poland is more historical. The most famous attractions are the Wawel Castle and the beautiful Old Town, with its enormous market place. There isn't ³*anything / nothing / something* more relaxing than sitting in the square, enjoying a cup of coffee. Walking through the narrow streets of the city, you'll find ⁴*anything / everything / something* old, strange or amazing around every corner.

To see ⁵*anything / everything / nothing* in the city you need to spend at least a week there, but you should choose your time to visit carefully. ⁶*Anybody / Everybody / Somebody* goes to Krakow in the summer, so from June to September, you might not find ⁷*anywhere / everywhere / somewhere* to stay.

⁸*Anyone / No one / Someone* who visits Krakow is disappointed with their holiday.

I can …	Very well	Quite well	More practice
talk about holidays.	○	○	○
use *something, anyone, everybody, nowhere,* etc.	○	○	○

49

7.3 Vocabulary development

Vocabulary -ed and -ing adjectives

> **STUDY TIP** -ed adjectives are formed from verbs and they follow the same rules as regular past simple forms. When the infinitive of the verb ends in /t/ or /d/, it has an extra syllable /ɪd/ in the past tense.

1 Tick (✓) the sentences that are correct and put a cross (✗) if they are wrong. Correct the incorrect sentences.
1 Paris is one of my favourite cities. The Eiffel Tower is amazing. ✓
2 I fell down the stairs. It was really embarrassed. ✗ *embarrassing*
3 The film was really disappointed. We didn't really enjoy it. _____
4 I'm really exciting about my sister's news. She's getting engaged! _____
5 There was a terrible storm last night. I was really frightened. _____
6 I heard some surprised news. I didn't expect it. _____
7 My neighbour called the police. He was worried about his son. _____
8 You look very relaxing. Have you been on holiday? _____

2 Complete the adjectives with -ed or -ing.
1 A Why do you always go to the swimming pool?
   B Because I find it very relax*ing*.
2 A Why aren't you talking to your boyfriend?
   B Because I'm annoy____ with him.
3 A Why did your friends go to bed?
   B Because they were tir____.
4 A Why are you watching that documentary again?
   B Because it's fascinat____.
5 A Why did you run out of the room?
   B Because I was embarrass____.
6 A Why are you looking at me like that?
   B Because I'm amaz____ that you passed.
7 A Why won't your girlfriend watch the football?
   B Because she thinks it's bor____.
8 A Why can't you do the homework?
   B Because I'm confus____.

Vocabulary review

3 Complete the transport words in the table.

advance   jams   pass   ~~road~~   transport

Car	Bus / Train
fuel	bus ³_____
main ¹ *road*	convenient
pollution	crowded
traffic ²_____	fare
	greener
	in ⁴_____
	public ⁵_____
	reliable

4 Match verbs 1–7 to words a–g to make verb phrases.
1 apply   a the area
2 buy   b for a visa
3 choose   c by the pool
4 explore   d your accommodation
5 go   e online reviews
6 lie   f travel insurance
7 read   g sightseeing

5 Complete the -ed and -ing adjectives.
1 *a*m*a*zed / ing
2 b_red / ing
3 d_s_pp__nted / ing
4 _xc_ted / ing
5 fr_ght_ned / ing
6 s_rpr_sed / ing
7 w_rried / ying
8 _nn_yed / ing
9 c_nf_sed / ing
10 _mb_rrassed / ing
11 f_sc_nated / ing
12 r_l_xed / ing

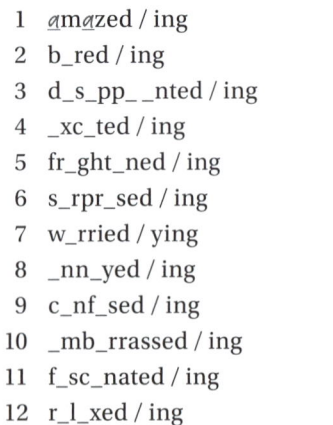

50 | Oxford 3000™

7.4 Speaking and writing

Speaking checking into a hotel

1a Put the conversation in the right order 1–11.

___ Thanks a lot.
___ You have to vacate your room by 10.30.
___ OK, Ms Genieva. So that's a single room just for one night.
_1_ Hi, I'd like to check in, please.
___ Right. Is there anywhere I can leave my luggage tomorrow?
___ Yeah, that's right.
___ Yes, my name's Tatiana Genieva.
___ Could you fill in the registration form, please?
___ Yes, of course. Do you have a reservation?
___ Yeah, sure. Just one question. What time is check-out?
___ Yes, you can leave it behind reception.

b 7.4))) Listen and check your answers to exercise **1a**.

2 Complete the conversation with the phrases in the box.

> ~~Could we check in, please?~~ I'll get someone to help you with your luggage. Is Wi-Fi available in the room? Is there a charge for it? What was the name again, please?

A Hi. [1] _Could we check in, please?_
B Yes, of course. What's the name, please?
A Anders. We have a reservation for four nights.
B [2] _____
A Anders. That's A-N-D-E-R-S.
B Right, Mr Anders. You're in Room 304. Here's your key card.
A Thanks. Just a few questions.
  [3] _____
B Yes, it is.
A Right.
  [4] _____
B No, it's free of charge to all our guests.
A Thanks. Can you tell me where the lift is?
B Yes, it's through those doors.
  [5] _____
A Thank you.

Writing short notes and messages

3 Put the words in the correct order to make short notes or messages.

1 text / your / for / Thanks / . / feeling / Am /better / much
   Thanks for your text. Am feeling much better.

2 work / Just / left / . / pizzas / me / Want / to get / some / dinner / for ?
   _____

3 traffic jam / in / Stuck / a / . / meeting / Will / late / be / for .
   _____

4 order / out / Lift / of / . / stairs / Use .
   _____

5 you / See / airport / at / Fri / on / . / 6.30 / lands / at / Plane .
   _____

6 client / Am / with / . / call / back / Will / mins / in / 15 .
   _____

I can …	Very well	Quite well	More practice
understand and use -ed and -ing adjectives.	○	○	○
check into a hotel.	○	○	○
write short notes and messages.	○	○	○

8 Language and learning

8.1 The amazing human brain

Grammar ability (*can, be able to*)

1a Replace the words in **bold** using *be able to*.
1. **My sister can't walk** because she has broken her leg.
   My sister isn't able to walk because she has broken her leg.
2. **Can you lend me some money** to go to a concert?
   _____
3. **I can drive** but I haven't got a car.
   _____
4. **We can see the sea** from the window of our room.
   _____
5. **Can your boyfriend speak** any foreign languages?
   _____
6. I'm tired because **I can't sleep at night**.
   _____

PRONUNCIATION *to* in *be able to*

b 8.1))) Listen and check. Notice the weak /tə/ pronunciation of *to* in each sentence.

c 8.1))) Listen again. Pause the CD and repeat after each sentence.

2 Complete the sentences with *can* or *can't* where possible. If not, use *be able to* in the correct form.
1. I *can* cook, but not as well as my mother.
2. I _____ finish your book by the end of the week, I'm sorry.
3. My nephew _____ play chess very well – he has won several competitions.
4. My grandparents _____ use a computer. They have never learnt.
5. Oh no, it's raining! We _____ have a barbecue tonight.
6. We _____ afford to go on a holiday this year, because we haven't got enough money.

3 Complete the text with *can, can't* or the correct form of *be able to* with the verbs in brackets.

Preparing for the future

Scientists say that there are many ways we [1] *can keep* (keep) our brains healthy, so that we [2] _____ (have) a normal life when we are older.

Learn a new activity

Think of something that you [3] _____ (not do) but you would like to learn: another language perhaps, or a musical instrument. Learning something new exercises your brain, so that you [4] _____ (deal) better with new situations in the future.

Do some exercise

A healthy body means a healthy brain. Doctors say that regular exercise might [5] _____ (stop) the brain getting ill with Alzheimer's, for example. People who don't go walking, running or swimming might have problems in later life because they [6] _____ (sleep).

Have fun

Going out with friends and spending time with relatives [7] _____ (make) you feel more positive about life. As you grow older, you will do different things together, but if you have friends, you [8] _____ (phone) someone for a chat at any time of the day.

Listen to the silence

You don't have to be active all of the time, and it is important to find a moment when you [9] _____ (relax). Our brains need time to rest, as well as our bodies, so that we don't feel stressed. This also prepares us for the future, when we [10] _____ (not go out) every day.

Vocabulary: skills and abilities

4 Complete the table with the phrases in the box.

| I'm brilliant I'm good I'm not very good ~~I'm OK~~ |
| I'm quite good I'm really good I'm very good |
| I'm terrible I'm useless |

++++		
+++		
++		
+	I'm OK	
−		
− −		

5 Use the words to write sentences.

1 My girlfriend / quite good / make speeches.
   My girlfriend is quite good at making speeches.
2 You / very good / tell jokes.
3 She / brilliant / organize events.
4 I / not very good / solve computer problems.
5 My husband / terrible / remember people's names.
6 They / good / spell.
7 I / OK / follow instructions.
8 We / useless / make decisions.
9 My daughter / really good / learn languages.
10 I / useless / telling jokes.

6 Complete paragraphs 1–4 with the adjectives in brackets and the correct form of the verbs in the box. Then match the paragraphs to the photos a–d. Write the letter of the photo in the space.

| explain fix follow give learn make organize |
| ~~remember~~ solve take tell understand |

1 He's *quite good at remembering* people's names (quite good), but he _____ computer problems (useless). He _____ things clearly (very good). Photo ___
2 She _____ events (good), but she _____ languages (not very good). She _____ speeches (very good). Photo ___
3 He _____ how things work (very good) and he _____ directions (OK). He _____ things that are broken (really good). Photo ___
4 She _____ instructions (quite good) but she _____ jokes (terrible). She _____ care of people (brilliant). Photo ___

I can …	Very well	Quite well	More practice
talk about ability.	○	○	○
talk about skills and abilities.	○	○	○

53

8.2 The secrets of a successful education

Vocabulary & Speaking education

1 Complete the crossword with school subjects.

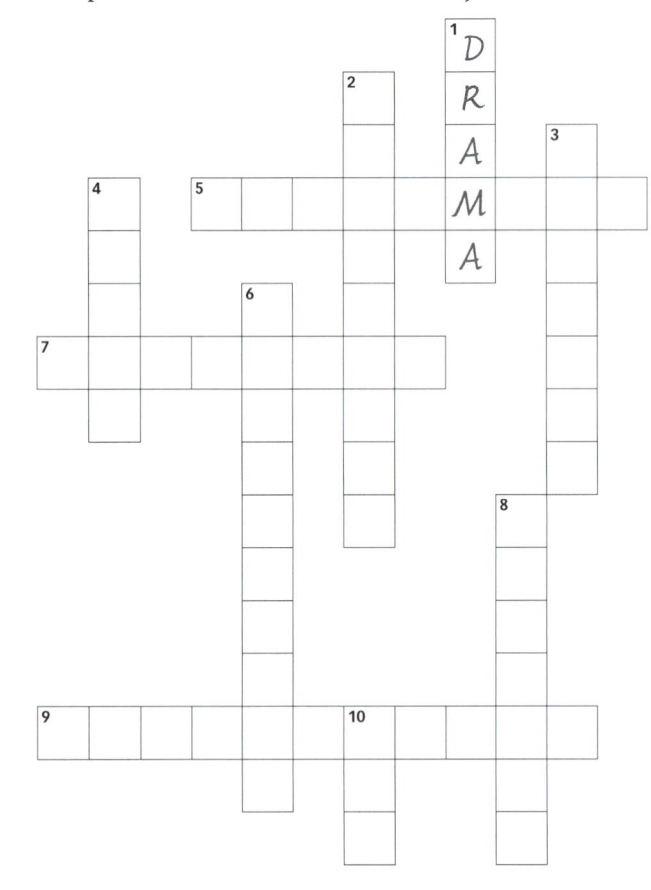

1 Students learn about plays and theatre in _drama_.
2 They study _____ like French and German, etc.
3 They learn about the physical world and nature in _____.
4 They study numbers, quantities and shapes in _____.
5 They learn about business and industry in _____.
6 They read different books in _____.
7 They play different sports in _____ education.
8 They learn about the past in _____.
9 They learn about computers in _____ technology.
10 They learn how to draw and paint in _____.

2 Complete the words in the sentences.
1 How often did you t_ake_ ex_ams_ when you were at school?
2 My brother loves travelling, so he'd like to tr_____ as a tour guide.
3 What qu_____ do you need if you want to be a lawyer?
4 Are you going to do a M_____ d_____ when you finish your course?
5 My teachers were very r_____ about homework and we only did it if we wanted to.
6 You have to get good gr_____ if you want to go to university.
7 I'm fascinated by the brain, so I'd like to study ps_____.
8 Parents don't have to pay to send their child to a st_____ sch_____.
9 My partner is studying at college for a d_____ in hotel management.

3 Complete the article with the words in the box.

| career | degree | do well | education | ~~private school~~ |
| strict | success | uniform | | |

Big is beautiful

With 47,000 students, City Montessori School in India is the largest school in the world. Parents pay £12 a month for younger students and £30 for older ones, which makes it a ¹ _private school_. The school rules are quite ²_____, and students have to wear a ³_____. Dr Jagdish Gandhi and Dr Bharti Ghandhi started the school in 1959, because they believed that all children have a right to an ⁴_____. Students say that they have to work very hard to ⁵_____, because there are a lot of students in each class. Most classes have between 40 and 50 students, but the teachers are happy with that number. As well as subjects such as Maths and English, students at City Montessori School learn about world peace. People in the local area like the school's philosophy, which is one of the reasons for its ⁶_____. On leaving school, some students have gone to do a ⁷_____ at Harvard University in the USA, while others have started a ⁸_____ at the United Nations.

54 Oxford 3000™

Grammar obligation, necessity and permission (*must, have to, can*)

PRONUNCIATION *can/can't*

4a 8.2))) Listen to the sentences and underline the words that are stressed.
1 You can <u>use</u> the <u>internet</u>.
2 You can't take photos.
3 You can sit here.
4 You can't walk on the grass.
5 You can pay by credit card.
6 You can't play football here.

b 8.2))) Listen again. Pause the CD and repeat after each sentence. Pay attention to the weak /kən/ pronunciation of *can* and the strong /kɑ:nt/ pronunciation of *can't*.

5 Choose the correct option to complete the sentences. In some sentences both answers may be possible.
1 We *don't have to* / *mustn't* go to work tomorrow. It's a holiday.
2 I'm late for a meeting. I *have to* / *must* go now.
3 Don't worry about the bill. We *can* / *must* pay by credit card.
4 There's a red flag. We *can't* / *mustn't* go swimming.
5 You *don't have to* / *mustn't* touch the cooker. It's hot.
6 You *can* / *have to* drive on the left in the UK.
7 You *must* / *have to* wear a seatbelt when you travel by car.
8 I *can't* / *don't have to* send personal emails from work.

6 Complete the article with the correct form of *must, have to* or *can* and the verbs in brackets. Sometimes there is more than one possible correct answer.

The world's smallest classroom

Sauder School of Business at the University of British Columbia in Vancouver, Canada, has given one of its teachers an unusual job for the day. Marketing Professor David Hardisty ¹ <u>has to give</u> (give) a class in an office block outside the university. But he ² _____ (not teach) students in a classroom. His 'students' are businessmen and women, and his 'classroom' is the lift of the building. Professor Hardisty ³ _____ (prepare) the lift to look like a classroom before everybody comes to work. He ⁴ _____ (not be) shy when the first people get into the lift, because he hasn't got much time to give the class. Instead he ⁵ _____ (start) talking as soon as the lift doors close. He ⁶ _____ (not relax) until his students get out on the top floor of the building. Then, he ⁷ _____ (get out) of the lift and watch the video of the class, which someone has filmed. Professor Hardisty ⁸ _____ (not do) the class every day because the university now has the video. They are going to put the video of the class onto the internet to advertise the business school.

I can ...	Very well	Quite well	More practice
talk about education.	○	○	○
talk about obligation, necessity and permission.	○	○	○

8.3 Vocabulary development

Vocabulary — make and do

> **STUDY TIP** Have a page in your vocabulary notebook for phrases with *make* and another for phrases with *do*. Each time you come across a new phrase with *make* or *do*, write it on the correct page. You could also make cards and test yourself from time to time. This will make it easier for you to remember which verb to use.

1 Choose the correct option to complete the sentences.
1. I *do* / *make* my English homework the night before the class.
2. Do you know where I can *do* / *make* a photocopy?
3. When was the last time you *did* / *made* an exam?
4. He *did* / *made* the exercise wrong so he has to repeat it.
5. We didn't *do* / *make* much money when we sold our car.
6. My partner is *doing* / *making* a job he hates.
7. My neighbours *did* / *made* a lot of noise last night.
8. I hope I've *done* / *made* the right decision.

2 Complete the conversations with *do* or *make* and the words or phrases in the box.

> a course   a list   a mistake   a salad   friends   housework
> nothing   well   your bed

1. **A** Did you _do a course_ in science at university?
   B No, I studied languages.
2. **A** Do you _____ before you go shopping?
   B Yes, I always write down what I have to buy.
3. **A** Do you _____ every morning?
   B Yes, I do it as soon as I get up.
4. **A** Do you ever _____ for lunch?
   B No, I usually have a sandwich.
5. **A** Do you ever have time to sit down and _____?
   B No, I'm always busy.
6. **A** How easy is it to _____ where you live?
   B It's easy. Everybody is really sociable.
7. **A** Do you always _____ in exams?
   B Yes, I usually pass.
8. **A** How often do you _____ in an email?
   B Quite often. I'm not very good at spelling.
9. **A** When do you usually _____?
   B I always clean my flat at the weekend.

Vocabulary review

3 Match words 1–7 to words a–g to form abilities.
1. explaining — a languages
2. following — b events
3. learning — c instructions
4. making — d things clearly
5. organizing — e jokes
6. solving — f speeches
7. telling — g computer problems

4 Complete the expressions for 'doing well' and 'doing badly'.

> ~~brilliant~~   good   OK   really   terrible

doing well
be [1] _brilliant_ at
be (quite / [3] _____ / very) good at
be [5] _____ at

doing badly
be [2] _____ / useless at
be not very [4] _____ at

5 Complete the missing vowels.

school subjects
1. _a_rt   drama
2. _c_n_m_cs
3. _T (_nf_rm_t__n t_chn_l_gy)
4. P_ (phys_c_l _d_c_t__n)

education
5. d_pl_m_
6. M_st_r's d_gr__
7. qu_l_f_c_t__ns
8. s_cc_ss
9. _n_f_rm

6 Complete the table with the words in the box.

> ~~business~~   a decision   an exam   friends   homework
> a job   a list   money   a phone call   well/badly

do	make
[1] _business_	[6] _____
[2] _____	[7] _____
[3] _____	[8] _____
[4] _____	[9] _____
[5] _____	[10] _____

Oxford 3000™

8.4 Speaking and writing

Speaking asking for clarification

1 Match sentences and questions 1–6 to responses a–f.
  1 Sorry, what did you say?   a Nothing. I'll explain later.
  2 What do you mean by   b Never mind. I'll draw you
    'a problem'?   a map.
  3 Sorry, I keep losing   c I said, I'm going to be late.
    the signal.
  4 I'm afraid I can't follow   d I said, do you come here
    your directions.   often?
  5 Sorry, what was that?   e Can I call back later?
  6 Sorry, I'm a bit confused.   f Don't worry. I'll say it
                                     again.

2a Complete the conversation with the phrases in the box.

> a really bad connection   breaking up   could you speak up
> I'm a bit lost   Pardon   Please could you explain
> repeat that please   noisy in here

A Raz? Where are you?
B Hi, Amara. I'm on my way.
A ¹ _Pardon_ ?
B I'm on my way.
A Sorry, it's too
  ² _____.
  Are you on your way? The
  party started an hour ago.
B Amara, I'm nearly there. But
  I've forgotten your address.
A Sorry, Raz. You're ³ _____. Can you
  remember my address?
B No, that's the problem.
A Raz, please ⁴ _____?
B OK. IS THAT BETTER?
A Yes, that's much better. I said can you remember my
  address? It's number 107.
B Could you ⁵ _____?
A 1-0-7. A hundred and seven South View Avenue.
B Right. ⁶ _____ how to get there from
  the bus stop?
A OK. When you get off the bus, walk up the hill and take
  the second right.
B Amara, this is ⁷ _____.
A Up the hill and second right. Did you get that?
B Sorry, ⁸ _____.
A Raz. Raz? He's gone.

b 8.3))) Listen and check your answers to the conversation in
  exercise 2a.

Writing completing a form

3 Complete the form with the words in the box.

> Date of birth   Forename   Gender   Marital status
> Next of kin   Occupation   Place of birth   Signature
> Surname   ~~Title~~

1 _Title_	Ms
2 _____	Larsson
3 _____	Agnetha
4 _____	Female
5 _____	22.09.1966
6 _____	Stockholm, Sweden
7 _____	Married
8 _____	Doctor
9 _____	Bjorn Larsson (husband)
10 _____	Agnetha Larsson

I can …	Very well	Quite well	More practice
use *make* and *do*.	○	○	○
understand connected speech.	○	○	○
ask for clarification.	○	○	○
complete a form.	○	○	○

8.5 Listening for pleasure

Frightening experiences

1 Label the photos with the words in the box.

fire   landing   passengers   ~~roundabout~~   snow

1 roundabout
2 _____
3 _____
4 _____
5 _____

2 8.4))) Listen to seven speakers describing their most frightening experience.

3 8.4))) Listen again and complete the summaries.

Speaker 1 was frightened because of the weather. She was going to visit her ¹ _mother-in-law_ and it was ² _____.

Speaker 2 was travelling by ³ _____. He nearly had an accident with a ⁴ _____ at a roundabout.

Speaker 3 was staying at a ⁵ _____. She had to leave her room because there was a ⁶ _____.

Speaker 4 was travelling by ⁷ _____. He was frightened because the pilot couldn't ⁸ _____.

Speaker 5 was sitting on a ⁹ _____. Another passenger made her give him her ¹⁰ _____.

Speaker 6 was ¹¹ _____ in the sea. One of his friends told him not to ¹² _____.

Speaker 7 was frightened by her ¹³ _____ having problems eating. Luckily, her ¹⁴ _____ helped.

4 Think about the speakers' frightening experiences again – which one did you think was the most scary? Why?

Review: Units 7 and 8

Grammar

1 Complete the sentences with one word. Sometimes more than one answer may be possible.

1. I was late for work this morning because I _couldn't_ start my car.
2. I don't know how I'm getting home, but I _____ get a taxi.
3. _____ is going on holiday, so there's a lot of traffic.
4. I'm sure your parents _____ enjoy their holiday – they love the beach.
5. You _____ park here because there is a 'No parking' sign.
6. I'm not doing _____ special this weekend.
7. We were _____ to find some cheap flights on the internet.
8. You _____ have a visa to enter the USA.

2 Choose the correct options to complete the text.

Public transport is getting more expensive **1** *anywhere / everywhere / nowhere / somewhere* in the world, but the metro of Beijing is doing **2** *anything / everything / nothing / something* that will make it much cheaper. In the stations of line 10, there are some brand new machines where passengers **3** *can / might / must / will* pay the fare with empty water bottles. To use the machine, you **4** *can / might / must / will* have a Beijing transport pass and at least one plastic bottle. For each recycled bottle, the machine **5** *can / might / must / will* put a small amount of money on the pass. You **6** *are able / can / have / must* to wait about 20 seconds for the machine to do its job, which **7** *can / have to / might / must* be too long for passengers on their way to work.

Vocabulary

3 Complete the sentences with a suitable word.

1. The underground is very _crowded_ in the morning and you can never get a seat.
2. My sister is very good at l_____ l_____, so she wants to be an interpreter.
3. Do you ever b_____ s_____ to help you remember your holiday?
4. My boyfriend is u_____ at remembering people's names.
5. Do you g_____ f_____ c_____ at the airport or from a bank?

4 Complete the article with the phrases in the box.

fuel   greener   lie by the pool   organizing events
~~pollution~~   science   trained

Flying causes a lot of **1** _pollution_, but that doesn't stop people going abroad when they want to **2** _____ of a hotel for a week. But now two Swiss scientists have designed a plane that they hope will help save the planet. Bertrand Piccard and Andre Borschberg were both fascinated by **3** _____ when they were at school, and they soon started building their own planes. They have both **4** _____ as pilots to be able to fly their inventions. Their latest model, Solar Impulse 2, gets its energy from the sun, which makes it much **5** _____ than other planes. It flies without using any **6** _____ at all. Piccard and Borschberg are planning to test their plane soon. They are also **7** _____ to teach people about this clean technology.

5 Choose the correct option to complete the sentences.

1. What's wrong with your car? It's *doing /* (*making*) a strange noise.
2. Were you *frightened / frightening* during the storm?
3. What has been the most *embarrassed / embarrassing* moment of your life?
4. What's the most interesting course you have ever *done / made*?
5. Did you *do / make* friends easily when you were a child?

Speaking

6 Complete the conversation with the phrases in the box.

could we check in, please   is Wi-Fi available in the room
could you fill in the registration form, please
~~Do you have a reservation~~
what do you mean by 'electronic device'

A Good morning. **1** _Do you have a reservation?_
B Yes, we do. **2** _____?
A Of course. What's the name, please?
B It's Sarilaksana.
A Here it is: Mr and Mrs Sarilaksana. **3** _____?
B Sure. One question: **4** _____?
A Yes, there's a connection in all of the rooms. I'll give you a code and you have to write it on your electronic device.
B **5** _____?
A That's your mobile phone, tablet or laptop computer.
B Thank you.

59

9 Body and mind

9.1 The rise and fall of the handshake

Vocabulary body and actions

1 Match verbs 1–10 to definitions a–j.

1	bump	a	push something with a part of your body
2	clap	b	move your mouth to show that you are happy
3	hug	c	show part of your body
4	kiss	d	touch somebody with your lips
5	nod	e	hit a part of your body against something
6	press	f	move quickly from side to side or up and down
7	shake	g	move your head up and down
8	smile	h	put your arms around somebody
9	stick out	i	put your hand or finger on somebody
10	touch	j	hit your hands together

2 Label the photo with the parts of the body in the box.

cheek chest chin elbow ~~forehead~~ lip shoulder thumb

1 forehead
2 ____
3 ____
4 ____
5 ____
6 ____
7 ____
8 ____

3 Complete the article with the words in the box.

cheek elbows ~~fist~~ hug nod shake smile touch

Body language around the world

When you are abroad, you must be careful how you express yourself with your body. If you make your hand into a ¹ _fist_ and begin to shake it at somebody, most people will understand that you're angry. But not all actions mean the same in every country.

In Asia, people are very careful not to ² _____ anybody with their foot. And, like many other countries, they never put their feet on chairs and tables where they are sitting.

In Fiji, people ³ _____ hands for a very long time. Don't worry if this continues for all of your conversation – it's normal.

Greetings in some European countries are often quite physical. People kiss friends and family on the ⁴ _____, and they often ⁵ _____.

In countries like France, what you do at the dinner table is very important. Don't put your ⁶ _____ on the table, and don't eat with your fingers. People will think you are rude if you do this.

Some countries have different ways of saying 'yes' and 'no'. In Greece and Bulgaria, people shake their head for yes and ⁷ _____ for no. This can be confusing, so it's probably better to learn the words for *yes* and *no*.

However, there is one international expression that everybody understands. If you are having problems and you don't know what to say, the best thing to do is ⁸ _____.

Grammar *if* + present simple, *will/won't/might*

4 Match the two halves of the sentences.
1. They'll think you're rude
2. Will he be angry
3. If you leave now,
4. Everything will be fine
5. If you make a mistake,
6. Will you translate for me
7. If you ask me nicely,
8. If I don't write it down

a you might miss the traffic.
b I won't remember it.
c if I don't shake his hand?
d it won't be the end of the world.
e I might help you.
f if you don't say *hello*.
g if you smile a lot.
h if I don't understand them?

5 Choose the correct option to complete the sentences.
1. If you *tell* / *'ll tell* me your secret, I *don't say* / *won't say* anything.
2. I *call* / *'ll call* you if I *get* / *'ll get* lost.
3. *Do you come* / *Will you come* to my wedding if I *invite* / *'ll invite* you?
4. If we *don't get up* / *won't get up* early, we *don't have* / *won't have* enough time.
5. I *get* / *might get* a taxi if we *finish* / *'ll finish* late.
6. *Do you enjoy* / *Will you enjoy* the holiday, if your partner *doesn't go* / *won't go*?
7. If you *don't speak* / *won't speak* the language, you *get* / *might get* bored.
8. It *is* / *'ll be* cheaper if we *go* / *'ll go* by bus.

PRONUNCIATION *'ll*

6a 9.1))) Listen to the pronunciation of *'ll*.

b 9.1))) Listen again. Pause the CD and repeat after each short form.

7 Complete the text with the correct form of the verbs in brackets.

Learning a language effectively

One of the best ways of learning a language is to spend some time in a country where people speak the language. If you ¹ _go_ (go) to Moscow, for example, you ² _____ (learn) Russian a lot more quickly than if you stay at home going to classes twice a week. It is probably better to go on this trip alone. If you ³ _____ (travel) in a group, you ⁴ _____ (spend) all your time speaking your own language with your friends.

Another option is to try and find a job abroad. If you ⁵ _____ (work) in a restaurant in Paris, for example, you ⁶ _____ (have to) speak French to the customers all day. Another idea is to share a flat with some people from the country. If you ⁷ _____ (find) a room in a shared flat in Berlin, for example, your German ⁸ _____ (be) fantastic by the time you go home. You could also try living with a family and looking after their children while you're away. The only problem is that you ⁹ _____ (feel) lonely if you ¹⁰ _____ (not go out) much. You ¹¹ _____ (not meet) anybody if you ¹² _____ (stay) in your room all day, so it's important to find somebody to talk to. If you ¹³ _____ (practise) the language a lot, you ¹⁴ _____ (feel) much more confident. Spending time abroad is a great experience, and you might not want to come home at the end of it!

I can ...	Very well	Quite well	More practice
talk about greetings.	○	○	○
talk about possible situations and the results.	○	○	○

61

9.2 Going back to nature

Vocabulary health and fitness

1 Complete the puzzle with words for health and fitness.

¹ W E I G H T L I F T I N G
 ² I
 ³ T
 ⁴ N
 ⁵ E
 ⁶ S
 ⁷ S

1 a sport in which people have to be very strong
2 small living things that can make you ill
3 always busy and doing a lot of things
4 a very dangerous illness
5 the food that you usually eat
6 serious illnesses
7 a feeling of worry because of problems in your life

2 Complete the words in the sentences.
1 Some people r_elax_ by reading or watching TV.
2 Crisps, burgers and pizzas are kinds of j_____ f_____.
3 Bad news can sometimes make you feel d_____.
4 Walking and swimming are kinds of g_____ e_____.
5 Colds and flu are different kinds of i_____.
6 F_____ is about being healthy and strong.
7 Meat, vegetables and fruit are kinds of n_____ f_____.
8 C_____ is a sport that you do with a bike.

3 Complete the text with the words in the box.

active cancer depressed diet diseases
fitness junk food ~~natural food~~

Seven-a-day

Many world governments today have realized the importance of eating ¹ _natural food_ and so they are recommending that people eat seven pieces of fruit and vegetables a day. They say that this will protect the body from dangerous ² _____, especially of the heart, and it may also stop people from getting illnesses such as ³ _____. Doctors have said that we need to look carefully at our ⁴ _____ if we want to stay healthy. They say that eating too much ⁵ _____ can make people fat, but it can also make them feel ⁶ _____. The wrong food can have a very negative effect on our mental health. People who eat healthily are generally more ⁷ _____ than those who do not, because they have more energy to do sport. The idea is that if we take our health and ⁸ _____ seriously by eating the right food and by doing the right exercise, we will be much happier when we are older and we will live longer.

PRONUNCIATION *eat* and *bread*

4a Look at the pairs of words. Put a tick (✓) if the pronunciation of *ea* is the same in each pair and put a cross (✗) if it is different.

1	eat	read	✓
2	bread	meat	✗
3	disease	dream	___
4	easy	weather	___
5	health	leather	___
6	already	instead	___
7	breakfast	team	___
8	cleaner	pleased	___

b 9.2))) Listen and check.

c 9.2))) Listen again. Pause the CD and repeat after each word.

Grammar present tenses in future time clauses

5 Choose the correct option to complete the sentences.
1 They'll be really pleased *before* / *if* / (*when*) they hear your good news.
2 You won't get the job *after* / *if* / *when* you don't speak good English.
3 He'll look for a new job *after* / *before* / *if* he comes back from his holiday.
4 She'll stay in bed again *as soon as* / *if* / *when* she doesn't feel better tomorrow.
5 We won't have time for breakfast *as soon as* / *before* / *if* we leave.
6 I'll call you *as soon as* / *before* / *if* I arrive at my hotel.

6 Use the words to write sentences about the future.
1 you / be late / if / you / not hurry up
   You'll be late if you don't hurry up.
2 I / call you / as soon as / I / get my results
   _____
3 we / be disappointed / if / our daughter / not go to university
   _____
4 they / go travelling / after / they / finish their course
   _____
5 she / talk to her boss / before / she / make a decision
   _____
6 we / not go to the party / if / we / not be invited
   _____
7 my son / learn to drive / when / he / be 18
   _____
8 you / not get better / if / you / not practise
   _____

7 Complete the leaflet with the correct form of the verbs in the box.

finish go not have not like see start tell ~~want~~

Change your life with yoga

Yoga is a great way to relax if you're feeling stressed, so why not try a class near you? Visit some of the studios in your area and choose the one which you like best. The teacher ¹ *will want* to talk to you when you sign up for a class. He or she will ask you some questions about your general health and fitness before you ² _____ for the first time. Find out if the studio has equipment. You might have to take your own if the studio ³ _____ any. On the first day, the instructor ⁴ _____ you where to stand when you enter the studio. Studios have their own rules, but you will probably need to turn off your mobile phone before the class ⁵ _____. Listen to the instructor and watch what the others are doing. The instructor will only come and help you if he or she ⁶ _____ that you are having problems. The first class is usually free and you won't have to go back if you ⁷ _____ it. But most people love yoga. You'll feel very relaxed after the class ⁸ _____. All you need to do then is to go home, have a nice hot shower and change into some comfortable clothes for the rest of the day.

I can …	Very well	Quite well	More practice
talk about health and fitness.	○	○	○
use present tenses in future time clauses.	○	○	○

9.3 Vocabulary development

Vocabulary — verbs and prepositions

> **STUDY TIP** Have a separate page in your vocabulary notebook for each preposition. Draw a mind map on the page. Every time you come across a verb which takes one of the prepositions, write it in the correct section. This will make it easier for you to remember which preposition to use.

1 Choose the correct option to complete the sentences.
 1 My partner works *for* / *on* / *to* a multinational company.
 2 I've always dreamt *of* / *in* / *on* having a big house by the sea.
 3 We might go camping at the weekend, but it depends *of* / *in* / *on* the weather.
 4 Can you think *in* / *of* / *on* somewhere nice to have dinner tonight?
 5 Did you succeed *in* / *of* / *on* passing all your exams?
 6 This jacket doesn't belong *for* / *of* / *to* me. Is it yours?

2 Complete the conversations with the correct form of the verbs in the box with the prepositions *for*, *in*, *of*, *on* or *to*.

> not believe   belong   consist   depend   succeed   think   work

 1 **A** Is this your apartment?
   B No, it _belongs to_ my parents. They let me use it in the summer.
 2 **A** What does your partner do?
   B She's a lawyer. She _____ _____ an international law firm.
 3 **A** What shall we get your mother for her birthday?
   B I don't know. I can't _____ _____ anything.
 4 **A** Do you think there is life on other planets?
   B No, I _____ _____ _____ aliens.
 5 **A** What time will we arrive?
   B I'm not sure. It _____ _____ the traffic.
 6 **A** What's Spanish omelette?
   B It's a dish that _____ _____ eggs and potatoes.
 7 **A** Why are you so happy?
   B I finally _____ _____ getting a job.

Vocabulary review

3 Complete the table with the body and action words in the box.

> chest   ~~clap~~   elbow   forehead   hug   nod   shake   shoulder   touch   tongue

actions	body
1 _clap_	6 _____
2 _____	7 _____
3 _____	8 _____
4 _____	9 _____
5 _____	10 _____

4 Complete the missing vowels in the health and fitness words.

 being ill [1] c_a_nc_e_r, diseases, [2] _lln_ss_s, viruses
 doing / not doing exercise [3] _ct_v_, cycling, [4] f_tn_ss, gentle exercise, [5] r_l_x, weightlifting
 eating [6] d__t, junk food, [7] n_t_r_l f__d
 mental health [8] d_pr_ss_d, stress

5 Complete the verbs with the prepositions in the box.

> for   in   of   on   to

 belong [1] _to_
 believe [2] _____
 consist [3] _____
 depend [4] _____
 dream [5] _____
 happen [6] _____
 succeed [7] _____
 think [8] _____
 work [9] _____

9.4 Speaking and writing

Speaking asking for help and giving advice

1 Put the conversation in the correct order 1–8.

- _1_ Hello. Please have a seat. Now, what can I do for you?
- ___ It's one tablet with meals three times a day. And you mustn't do any sport for a week.
- ___ Right. Thanks very much for your help.
- ___ Let me have a look. It isn't broken, but I don't think you should walk on it.
- ___ Yes, it hurts a lot. Could you give me something for the pain?
- ___ OK. How often should I take the tablets?
- ___ I've hurt my foot. I was playing football and I fell over.
- ___ Yes, I'll give you some painkillers. You could try putting ice on your foot, too.

2a Complete the conversation with the phrases in the box.

| It's a good idea | How can I help you? | I think you should |
| Have you got anything | you could try | You mustn't |

A Morning. ¹ _How can I help you?_
B Hello. ² _____ for a cold?
A Well, there isn't much I can do really.
   ³ _____ go home and get lots of rest.
B Can you give me something for my cough? It's very annoying.
A Yes, ⁴ _____ this medicine. Take it every six hours until the cough goes away.
B Right.
A ⁵ _____ to drink lots of water, too. And keep warm. ⁶ _____ go out.
B OK. Thank you very much.

b 9.3))) Listen and check your answers.

Writing a formal covering letter

3 Complete the letters with the words in the box.

| additional | Dear | details | enclose | enclosed | faithfully |
| hear | hearing | like | Madam | sincerely | wish |

¹ _Dear_ Mr Thompson

I ² _____ to apply for your MovNat course in the first week of June.

As requested, I ³ _____ my completed application form in English and a current medical certificate.

Please contact me if you require any ⁴ _____ information.

I hope to ⁵ _____ from you soon.

Yours ⁶ _____

Jens Schmidt

Dear Sir / ⁷ _____

I would ⁸ _____ to request a refund for the T-shirt that I purchased from your company.

Please find ⁹ _____ the T-shirt and my completed returns form.

Please inform me if you require any further ¹⁰ _____ .

I look forward to ¹¹ _____ from you.

Yours ¹² _____

Mitsuki Akimoto

I can …	Very well	Quite well	More practice
use verbs and prepositions.	○	○	○
ask for help and give advice.	○	○	○
write a formal covering letter.	○	○	○

10 Food

10.1 A question of taste

Vocabulary describing food

1 Complete the crossword from the clues below.

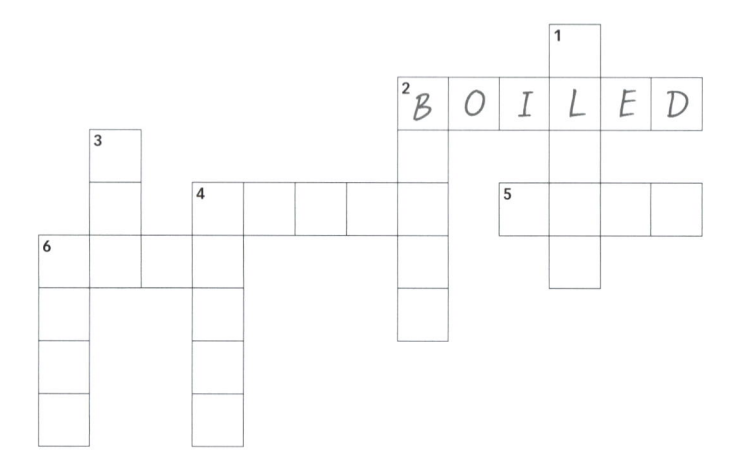

Across ▶
2 cooked in water heated to 100°C
4 food that you eat quickly between main meals
5 not having a strong taste
6 a dish made by cooking meat and vegetables in liquid for a long time

Down ▼
1 simple, not complicated
2 cooked in an oven on a dry heat
3 causing a burning feeling in your mouth
4 tastes as if it contains a lot of sugar
6 having a sharp taste like a lemon

2 Complete the descriptions and match sentences 1–4 to photos a–d.

1 We have this as a light m_eal_. It's m_____ with rice and it has r_____ fish in it. Photo ___
2 It's a s_____ of pie, but it's s_____, not sweet. It's made with eggs and small pieces of bacon. You can e_____ it hot or cold. Photo ___
3 It has cooked meat or vegetables and sp_____ in it. It t_____ quite hot. It's often s_____ with rice. Photo ___
4 It's a k_____ of dessert. It's made with some special cakes, but it has a b_____ taste because it h_____ coffee in it. Photo ___

3 Complete the menu with the words in the box.

dessert   fried   ~~herbs~~   honey   lamb   sauce   spicy   thick

Rosie's Kitchen

Starter
Potato soup with fresh ¹ _herbs_
² _____ prawns – quite hot!

Main course
Boiled ham with cheese ³ _____ and carrots
⁴ _____ fish with chips and peas
Roast ⁵ _____ with roast potatoes and mixed vegetables

⁶ _____
Apple pie with ⁷ _____ double cream
Greek yoghurt with ⁸ _____

Crossword: 2 across: BOILED

PRONUNCIATION number of syllables in words

4a Complete the table with the words in the box.

> ~~chocolate~~ different favourite
> interesting raspberry restaurant
> several strawberry temperature
> vegetable

Two-syllable words	Three-syllable words
chocolate	_____
_____	_____
_____	_____
_____	_____
_____	

b 10.1))) Listen and check.

c 10.1))) Listen again. Pause the CD and repeat after each word.

Grammar uses of the *-ing* form

5 Match the two halves of the sentences.
1 We're really looking forward to _b_
2 Is your boyfriend interested in ___
3 They ended the meal by ___
4 I really don't mind ___
5 Do you enjoy ___
6 The children haven't finished ___

a learning how to cook?
b giving our first dinner party.
c doing the washing up.
d eating their soup.
e ordering some coffee.
f going to concerts?

➡ **STUDY TIP** Make a note of any irregular *-ing* forms in your notebook, e.g. *write – writing, stop – stopping*. This will make it easier for you to remember the correct spelling.

6 Complete the sentences with the *-ing* form of the verbs in brackets. Then write **V** if the *-ing* form is after a verb, **P** after a preposition and **S** if it is used as a subject.
1 I hate _buying_ food at the weekend. The supermarket is always full. (buy) _V_
2 _____ a large meal can make you feel sleepy. (have) ___
3 This dessert is delicious! I could go on _____ it forever. (eat) ___
4 We get most of our vegetables by _____ our own food. (grow) ___
5 I don't feel like _____ tonight. Let's go out for dinner. (cook) ___
6 _____ eight glasses of water a day is good for your health. (drink) ___
7 I always buy birthday cakes because I'm not very good at _____ them. (make) ___
8 _____ food in the microwave is quicker than putting it in the oven. (heat) ___
9 Kate is worried about _____ her husband's family for a meal. (invite) ___

7 Complete the article with the *-ing* form of the verbs in the box.

> eat finish get ~~go~~ know prepare serve tell try

The very best food

What do you think about ¹ _going_ to Michelin-starred restaurants? It is only the very best restaurants that have a Michelin star, but you can find them all over the world. It is true that they are more expensive than usual and the bill often comes to hundreds of pounds, but foodies love ² _____ at these restaurants. ³ _____ the dishes is often a wonderful experience because the chefs have spent hours ⁴ _____ each one of them. There are usually a lot of chefs in the kitchen, and each one is responsible for one of the dishes on the menu.

⁵ _____ a Michelin star is a great honour for a restaurant, because it means that the head chef is one of the best in the profession. Michelin inspectors visit restaurants without ⁶ _____ anybody that they are coming, so that the chefs cannot make any special preparations. But usually, the chef has an idea that an inspector is in the area because a chef from another restaurant tells him or her. After ⁷ _____ their meal, the inspector pays the bill and leaves, like all the other customers. It is only later that the chef finds out his or her opinion of the restaurant. ⁸ _____ that perhaps they are cooking for a Michelin inspector can make chefs very nervous. They usually prefer ⁹ _____ normal customers, who do not have to make such an important decision about the food.

I can ...	Very well	Quite well	More practice
describe a national dish.	○	○	○
use the *-ing* form.	○	○	○

67

10.2 Canned dreams

Vocabulary food containers

1 Find eight food and drink containers in the word search.

B	O	C	A	B	O	X	T	K	T
O	P	J	A	O	C	K	E	L	A
C	C	A	R	T	O	N	B	O	S
R	J	R	E	T	U	B	E	R	O
O	C	T	R	L	I	N	J	N	R
P	A	C	K	E	T	F	C	B	X
D	N	T	I	R	I	B	U	F	U
C	A	J	A	T	N	R	S	T	P

2a Complete the shopping list for a summer party.

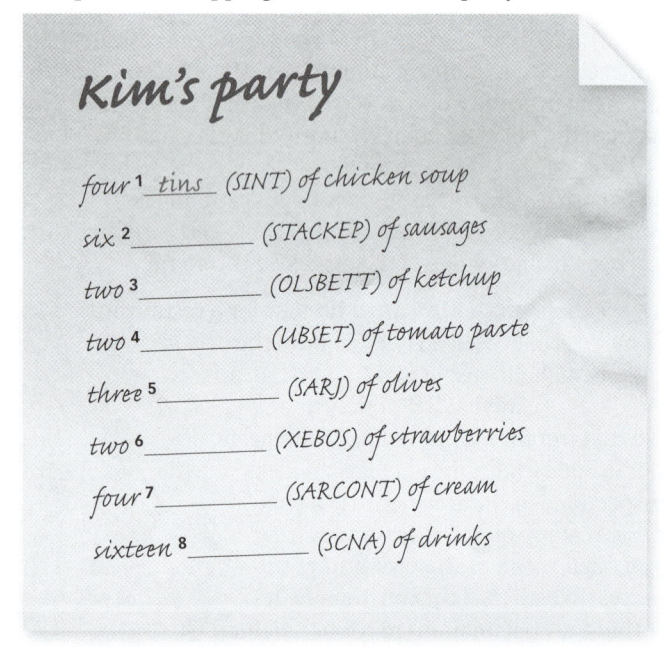

Kim's party

four ¹ _tins_ (SINT) of chicken soup
six ² _____ (STACKEP) of sausages
two ³ _____ (OLSBETT) of ketchup
two ⁴ _____ (UBSET) of tomato paste
three ⁵ _____ (SARJ) of olives
two ⁶ _____ (XEBOS) of strawberries
four ⁷ _____ (SARCONT) of cream
sixteen ⁸ _____ (SCNA) of drinks

b 10.2))) Listen and check.

c 10.2))) Listen and repeat the phrases in exercise 2a.

3 Complete the article with the words in exercise 1.

Space food

Eating in space is much more difficult than it is on Earth because food does not stay in one place. Astronauts can only have 1.7 kilograms of food per person per day, so the size and weight of the container is important. You won't find a ¹ _jar_ of jam or a glass ² _____ of water on the International Space Station because glass is too heavy. You won't see a ³ _____ of apples either, because fresh fruit doesn't last very long.

In the past, all of the food in space had the same texture as toothpaste, and astronauts had a ⁴ _____ of food at each meal. Now things have changed and most of the containers are made of plastic. However, some food is the same as it is at home, and perhaps once a week, it is possible to have a ⁵ _____ of tuna or a ⁶ _____ of ham for lunch.

Drinking is also more difficult in space. Most drinks come in plastic cups, and astronauts have to add cold or hot water to the cup. You won't find a ⁷ _____ of lemonade or a ⁸ _____ of juice anywhere in space.

Oxford 3000™

Grammar the passive

4 Choose the correct option to complete the sentences.
1. Most people in China *drink* / *is drunk* tea.
2. The chef *didn't cook* / *weren't cooked* the potatoes enough.
3. The pizzas *delivered* / *were delivered* to our house.
4. We *ate* / *were eaten* sushi for lunch yesterday.
5. Cans *don't make* / *aren't made* of plastic.
6. Hamburgers *didn't invent* / *weren't invented* in the USA.
7. You *don't use* / *aren't used* pasta to make paella.
8. Coffee *produces* / *is produced* in Brazil.

5 Use the words to write present or past passive sentences.
1. eggs / pack / in boxes of six or twelve
   Eggs are packed in boxes of six or twelve.
2. rice / not grow / in cold places
3. this bread / bake / yesterday
4. meals / not eat / in front of the TV when I was young
5. milk / not sell / in cartons in the past
6. toast / make / with bread
7. those apple trees / plant / last year
8. olives / not usually serve / for dessert

6 Complete the article with the correct passive form of the verbs in brackets.

Pizza: the world's favourite dish

Millions of pizzas ¹ *are eaten* (eat) every day, but have you ever wondered where the pizza came from? In the 16th century, a kind of flat bread called 'pizza' ² _____ (sell) on the streets of Naples. The bread was very plain and it ³ _____ (not buy) by many people, only the poor. Ingredients ⁴ _____ (not add) to this pizza until the middle of the 19th century, when the pizza became more popular. A few years later, one of the city's pizza makers tried out a new idea on the king's wife, Margherita of Savoy. He made a pizza with mozzarella cheese, tomatoes and herbs on top, and the queen loved it! The man's name was Raffaele Esposito and his experiment became known as the Pizza Margherita. Today, this pizza is typical in Naples, but only if it ⁵ _____ (prepare) by hand. There are a lot of rules telling chefs how to make traditional pizzas and machines ⁶ _____ (not use). Pizza makers have to use a special oven, too.

Pizzas ⁷ _____ (take) to other countries at the end of the 19th century by Italian immigrants looking for work. Some immigrants made pizzas at home to sell on the streets, while others opened pizzerias. Today, the pizza ⁸ _____ (not only serve) to customers in restaurants; people can call a restaurant to order a pizza to eat at home.

I can ...	Very well	Quite well	More practice
talk about food.	○	○	○
use the passive.	○	○	○

10.3 Vocabulary development

Vocabulary words with more than one meaning

1 Read the text and choose the correct meaning (a or b) for the words in *italics*.

> Do you know what a freegan is? It's a person who has found a completely new ¹ *way* of feeding their family. Freegans are against the high ² *figures* of wasted food in our society and so they are trying to do something about it. A freegan's ³ *diet* is made up of things that other people throw away. They find most of their food in the bins outside large supermarkets. Freegans often go there to wait for the products that are ⁴ *left* at the end of the day. They can often find vegetables with a few ⁵ *marks* or fruit that is a ⁶ *funny* shape. Supermarkets do not ⁷ *charge* freegans for the food they take, so all of their meals are completely free. And most of the products are safe because they aren't usually ⁸ *past* their sell-by date.

1 a distance — (b) method
2 a the shape of human bodies — b numbers
3 a food they normally eat — b food they eat to get thinner
4 a remaining, still there — b opposite of right
5 a spots that spoil something — b scores of a test or essay
6 a making you laugh — b strange
7 a ask them to pay a price — b put electricity into a battery
8 a later than — b the time before now

2 Complete the sentences with five of the words in exercise 1. Use the same word for each pair of sentences.

1 A Do you eat a healthy _____?
  B The doctor has told me to go on a _____.
2 A Throw that orange away. It looks a bit _____.
  B The waiter was really _____. He made us laugh.
3 A In the _____, this café used to be very popular.
  B Do you ever eat yoghurts that are _____ their sell-by date?
4 A The eggs are at the back of the shop on the _____.
  B It's nearly closing time, so there isn't any bread _____.
5 A There's a strange _____ on that apple. Don't eat it.
  B What _____ would you give the meal – a seven?

Vocabulary review

3 Complete the missing vowels in the food words.

how it is eaten	¹ b<u>a</u>k<u>e</u>d, boiled, ² fr__d, raw
ingredients	herbs, ³ h_n_y, lamb, ⁴ sp_c_s
taste and texture	⁵ b_tt_r, hot/spicy, ⁶ m_ld, plain, ⁷ s_v__ry, sour, ⁸ sw__t, thick
type of dish	dessert, ⁹ s__ce, snack, ¹⁰ st_w

4 Match the two halves of the sentences.

1 It's a kind / sort of   a the summer.
2 It's made with   b delicious.
3 It has   c a starter.
4 People have this as   d soup.
5 You can eat it in   e garlic in it
6 It has a sour   f tomatoes and other vegetables.
7 It's often served   g taste.
8 It tastes   h with small pieces of tomato and onion.

5 Complete the phrases with the words in the box.

| ~~bottle~~ box can carton jar packet tin tube |

a ¹ _bottle_ of lemonade, vinegar, water
a ² _____ of tomato paste, toothpaste
a ³ _____ of cereal, chocolates, eggs
a ⁴ _____ of baby food, jam, olives
a ⁵ _____ of energy drink, fruit juice, lemonade
a ⁶ _____ of carrots, tomatoes, tuna
a ⁷ _____ of juice, milk, soup
a ⁸ _____ of crisps, frozen peas, rice

6 Complete the words.

1 ch_arge_   ask a price / put electricity into a battery
2 cl_____   obvious / something that you can see through
3 d_____   food you normally eat / food you eat to get thinner
4 f_____   a number / the shape of the human body
5 f_____   making you laugh / strange
6 l_____   opposite of right / remaining, still there
7 m_____   a spot that spoils the look of something / a score in a test or essay
8 p_____   later than / the time before now

10.4 Speaking and writing

Speaking — problems in a restaurant

1 Choose the correct phrase, *a*, *b* or *c*.

What do you say if …
1 there's a problem with your order?
   a I do apologize.
   b There seems to be a mistake. *(circled)*
   c Don't worry about it.
2 you want the waiter to give you something?
   a Would you mind bringing me another one?
   b It's not your fault.
   c You've charged us for two, but we've only had one.
3 you want to make an apology?
   a I'm afraid it's wrong.
   b Could you possibly change it?
   c I'm terribly sorry.

2a Decide if the conversations belong to Conversation 1 or Conversation 2. Write *1* or *2*.

_1_ **Customer (C)** Excuse me? I'm afraid I can't eat this steak. It's raw.
_2_ **C** Excuse me? Could you possibly bring me the bill?
___ **Waiter (W)** Yes, of course … Here it is.
___ **W** Really? I'll take it back to the kitchen for you.
___ **C** No, I'd like to order something else, please.
___ **C** Oh. There seems to be a mistake.
___ **W** Is there?
___ **W** Of course. What would you like?
___ **C** Yes. You've charged me for the steak, but I didn't eat it.
___ **C** I'm not sure. Would you mind bringing me the menu again?
___ **W** You're absolutely right. I do apologize.
___ **W** Of course not. I'm terribly sorry about your steak.
___ **C** Don't worry about it. Erm, I'll have a salad, please.
___ **C** Don't worry. It's not your fault.

b 10.3))) Listen and check.

Writing — a restaurant review

3 Tick (✓) the sentences where the apostrophe is used correctly and put a cross (✗) if it is wrong. Correct the incorrect sentences.

1 It's a great restaurant. ✓
2 It hasnt been open for long. ✗
   It hasn't been open for long.
3 The owners' wife greeted us at the door. ___
4 The waiter's were all very friendly. ___
5 The other diners' meals looked delicious. ___
6 My friend's and I will definitely go back. ___
7 They haven't changed the menu. ___
8 Hes forgotten the drinks. ___

4 Complete the review with the words in the box.

atmosphere   food   ~~location~~   service   value for money

LATERAL

I took my boyfriend to Lateral for his birthday yesterday, and we weren't disappointed. The ¹ _location_ of the restaurant is not ideal as it's in a very narrow street where it's difficult to park. But the place was busy and it had a very lively ² _____, so we didn't mind. The ³ _____ was excellent and the waiters and waitresses were all very helpful. But the best thing about the restaurant was the ⁴ _____. My prawns were delicious, and the vegetables were cooked perfectly. My boyfriend's fish was delicious too. I had a nice surprise when I asked for the bill as the price was very reasonable. We both thought the meal was fantastic ⁵ _____. We've already told all our friends about Lateral because we had such a good time.

I can …	Very well	Quite well	More practice
understand words with more than one meaning.	○	○	○
explain and deal with problems.	○	○	○
write a review of a restaurant.	○	○	○

10.5 Reading for pleasure

Making chocolate

1 Look at the photo of a cacao pod. Match words 1–4 to definitions a–d.

1	pod	a	the soft inside part of a pod
2	shell	b	the fruit of the cacao tree
3	pulp	c	the seeds of the cacao tree
4	beans	d	the hard outside part of a pod

2 Read an extract from a factfile.

3 Complete the summary.

> Cacao ¹_pods_ begin to grow when a tree is about ²_____ years old. When the pods change ³_____, people take them down and cut them open. First they put the cacao beans in large ⁴_____ covered with ⁵_____ leaves for up to a week. Then they dry the beans on large ⁶_____ in the sun for two or three weeks. After that, the farmers sell the beans to ⁷_____, who sell them on to ⁸_____ to be made into chocolate bars.

4 Think about the process of making chocolate. Did you know before how chocolate was made?

Do you like chocolate? Why/Why not? If so, which type of chocolate is your favourite?

From cacao pod to chocolate bar

The cacao tree begins to have its first pods after about three years. It is very different from most other trees because its flowers and then its pods grow from the centre of the tree.

The large cacao pods are wonderful to see. At first, they are a beautiful light green. But after six months, when they are ready to open, they become very colourful. They can be bright red or orange, dark purple or deep green.

The people on the plantation take down the pods with very long sticks. Then they cut them open with big knives. Inside they find between 20 and 40 cacao beans in the soft white pulp. The beans are very hard and they do not smell or taste like chocolate.

The workers then usually put the beans and the pulp in large boxes with some banana leaves on the top. They leave these in the hot sun for four to seven days and some of the chemicals in the beans begin to change.

The beans are now very different. They are no longer white or purple – they are dark brown. And very importantly, they smell of wonderful chocolate!

Next, the plantation workers put the beans onto large tables. They dry the beans in the sun for ten to twenty days and move them from time to time. On larger plantations they dry them in special buildings. But the best chocolate comes from beans which stay in the sun for a long time.

The farmers then put the beans into bags of about 64 kilograms each and sell them to brokers – business people who buy and sell cacao beans for money. The brokers then sell them to the chocolate factories. But the chocolate factories do not just buy one type of bean. Beans from different countries, or even from different factories, taste different. In the factories, people mix together different types of bean to get chocolate with just the right taste.

Text extract from *Oxford Bookworms Factfiles: Chocolate*

Review: Units 9 and 10

Grammar

1 Choose the correct option to complete the sentences.
1. Paella *is made* / *makes* / *is making* with rice.
2. The children *have* / *having* / *will have* a snack later if they get hungry.
3. We avoid *buy* / *buying* / *will buy* white bread because it's unhealthy.
4. We'll have dinner as soon as it *'ll be* / *'s* / *was* ready.
5. If it *doesn't rain* / *don't rain* / *won't rain*, we'll have a barbecue this weekend.
6. I'm going to give up *eat* / *eating* / *will eat* biscuits.
7. Before I *start* / *starting* / *will start* cooking today's lunch, I'll get changed.
8. Potatoes *are taking* / *took* / *were taken* to Europe in the sixteenth century.

2 Complete the text with the correct form of the verbs in brackets.

> ¹ *Growing* (grow) your own food does not have to be difficult, say the people of Todmorden. If you visit this town in the north of England, you ² _____ (not see) many people in the shops. This is because most of the residents prefer ³ _____ (eat) the food they grow. Todmorden is part of the 'Incredible Edible' project, which ⁴ _____ (start) by two women who live in the town. The group believes that if they ⁵ _____ (not prepare) for the future, there won't be enough food for everybody. Fruit and vegetables ⁶ _____ (plant) everywhere, there are even some lettuces outside the police station. But people grow things without ⁷ _____ (expect) anybody to pay for them. When food ⁸ _____ (begin) to disappear from the shops in the future, the people of Todmorden know they will be safe.

Vocabulary

3 Circle the word that is different.
1. clap   (fist)   kiss   nod
2. boiled   baked   depressed   fried
3. diseases   herbs   illnesses   viruses
4. cycling   fitness   forehead   weightlifting
5. active   bitter   sour   sweet
6. hug   greet   touch   tongue
7. box   dessert   jar   packet
8. elbow   shoulder   stress   thumb

4 Complete the text with the missing words.

> Goulash is one of the national dishes of Hungary, but it is also popular in Central and Southern Europe and Scandinavia. It's a ¹ s*avoury* dish, which is a main meal. Goulash is a kind of ² st_____ which is made with meat, such as beef or ³ l_____ and vegetables. It tastes quite ⁴ sp_____, because it has paprika in it. Different varieties of goulash can be made by adding a ⁵ c_____ of sour cream or a ⁶ t_____ of beans. In some countries, part of a ⁷ b_____ of tomato sauce or a ⁸ t_____ of tomato paste may also be used to make the goulash thicker.

5 Complete the sentences with the words in the box.

diet   funny   in   left   ~~mark~~   of   on   to

1. I don't want that apple – it has a *mark* on it.
2. Can you think _____ a nice restaurant where we can have dinner tonight?
3. I think I need to go on a _____ because my clothes feel uncomfortable.
4. We might have lunch in the garden, but it depends _____ the weather.
5. I don't believe _____ taking tablets to lose weight.
6. Throw that milk away if it tastes _____.
7. Can you get some eggs if you happen _____ remember?
8. I can't make you a sandwich because there isn't any bread _____.

Speaking

6 Put the words in the correct order to make sentences.
1. you / bed / should / I / in / think / stay
   I think you should stay in bed.
2. me / clean / possibly / you / plate / give / Could / a
   _____
3. heavy / mustn't / anything / You / lift
   _____
4. a / seems / the / There / in / be / bill / to / mistake
   _____
5. a / Have / throat / anything / you / for / got / sore
   _____
6. on / try / You / some / could / it / cream / putting
   _____

73

11 World

11.1 Making the world a better place

Vocabulary global issues

1 Match words 1–9 to definitions a–i.

1	advance	a	the state of somebody's body or mind
2	environment	b	putting scientific discoveries into practice
3	farming	c	the study of natural laws and the physical world
4	health	d	the state of being healthy and happy
5	population	e	something new in a particular field
6	science	f	the natural world around us
7	technology	g	the number of people that live in a place
8	unemployment	h	the number of people who cannot find a job
9	well-being	i	growing food and looking after animals

(1 matches to e)

2 Choose the correct option to complete the sentences.
1 Minis are made in a *shop / factory* in Oxford.
2 The new shopping centre will *create / spread* new jobs in the area.
3 The weather is changing because of *world / global* warming.
4 You can read about the facts and *numbers / figures* in the latest report.
5 Do you agree that money brings *happiness / happy*?
6 Scientists are hoping to find a *cure / treat* for cancer soon.
7 People have less money since the start of the financial *crisis / problem*.
8 Illnesses like flu *create / spread* very quickly.
9 World *hunger / hungry* affects many countries, especially those in Africa.

3 Complete the article with the words in the box.

environment factories facts financial ~~global~~ health
hunger situation unemployment warming

Cutting down on world pollution

The countries of the world sometimes meet to discuss ¹ *global* issues. Two of the most important meetings were the *Earth Summit* in Rio de Janeiro in 1992 and *Rio +20* in the same city in 2012. At the meetings, world leaders talked about different ways they could protect the ² _____. They looked at all the ³ _____ and figures from industry in different countries and agreed that ⁴ _____ shouldn't produce so much pollution. They hoped that this would slow down global ⁵ _____. They also looked at pollution from cars on the streets, which they say is bad for people's ⁶ _____. At the meeting, they recommended that cities should have more public transport, and people should stop using their cars. Some people think that governments should do more about the world's problems. They say that there is enough food for everybody, so world ⁷ _____ should not exist. Unfortunately, most people are worried about the economic ⁸ _____ in their own countries today. In many places, companies have closed because of the ⁹ _____ crisis, so many workers have lost their jobs. Today, ¹⁰ _____ is a problem in many countries, and it is a difficult one to solve.

Oxford 3000™

Grammar *if* + past tense + *would*

4a Put the words in the correct order to make sentences and questions.
1 a / I / work / would / I / car, / had / If / drive / to
   If _I had a car, I would drive to work._
2 be / job / wouldn't / I / my / if / I / happy / lost
   I _____.
3 time / you / What / in / go / if / do / could / you / back / would
   What _____?
4 she / him / his / knew / she'd / number, / If / call
   If _____.
5 you / if / choice / you / live / would / Where / the / had
   Where _____?
6 exercise / better / did / if / feel / you / 'd / some / You
   You _____.

PRONUNCIATION *if* + past tense + *would* sentences

b 11.1))) Listen to sentence 1 in exercise **4a**. Notice how the stressed words are underlined and the intonation is marked in the sentence.

If I had a <u>car</u>, I would <u>drive</u> to <u>work</u>.

c 11.2))) Listen to sentences 2–6 in exercise **4a**. Underline the stressed words and mark the intonation in the sentences.

d 11.2))) Listen again. Pause the CD and repeat after each sentence.

5 Complete the sentences with the correct form of the verbs in brackets.
1 If you _worked_ less, you _would have_ more free time. (work, have)
2 People _____ the country if unemployment _____ so high. (not leave, not be)
3 Where _____ you _____ on holiday if you _____ a lot of money? (go, have)
4 You _____ tired if you _____ so early. (not be, not get up)
5 We _____ a dog if we _____ in the country. (have, live)
6 If it _____, plants _____. (not rain, not grow)
7 I _____ the weekend more if I _____ on Saturdays. (enjoy, not work)
8 What _____ you _____ if you _____ your country's leader? (say, meet)

6 Complete the article with the correct form of the verbs in the box.

be   become   not eat   go   ~~happen~~   not need

EAT LESS MEAT

What ¹ _would happen_ if everybody in the world stopped eating meat? There is no question that humans eat far too much meat, but ² _____ it really _____ better if all of us were vegetarians? Every day, millions of people around the world work with animals on farms. If we all ³ _____ vegetarians, there would be fewer animals to look after. We would keep cows to give us milk and hens to give us eggs, but we ⁴ _____ as many farm workers. Where ⁵ _____ they _____ to find a new job? On the other hand, cows produce 18% of the world's greenhouse gases, so if we ⁶ _____ beef, it would be better for the environment. There are arguments for the world becoming vegetarian and arguments against it. Probably the best solution is to eat less meat, but not to stop eating it altogether.

I can ...   Very well   Quite well   More practice
talk about global issues.   ○   ○   ○
talk about unlikely situations in the future.   ○   ○   ○

75

11.2 Breaking news

Grammar *used to*

1a Use the words to make sentences with *used to*, *didn't use to* or *Did ... use to?*

1 my brother / work in a bank +
   My brother used to work in a bank.

2 we / not have a garden −
   _____

3 my parents / live in a flat +
   _____

4 you / have long hair ?
   _____

5 I / not drink coffee −
   _____

6 your boyfriend / have a motorbike ?
   _____

7 I / wear glasses +
   _____

PRONUNCIATION *to* in *used to*

b 11.3)) Listen and check. Pay attention to the weak pronunciation of *to* /tə/ in *used to*.

c 11.3)) Listen again and repeat the sentences.

2 Tick (✓) the sentences that are correct and put a cross (✗) if they are wrong. Correct the incorrect sentences.

1 I used to live with friends, but now I have my own flat. ✓

2 We didn't used to do anything at weekends, but now we go walking.
   ✗ We didn't use to do anything at weekends, but now we go walking.

3 What kind of music did you used to listen to when you were a teenager?
   _____

4 My parents used to be more active than they are now.
   _____

5 One day, we used to have a car accident.
   _____

6 They didn't used to eat fish, but now they prefer it to meat.
   _____

7 Our children not use to go out at night, but now they do.
   _____

3 Complete the article with the correct form of the verbs in the box. Use *used to*, *didn't use to* or *Did ... use to?*

| be   not happen   look   read   sit   not smile   ~~watch~~ |
| not work |

¹ *Did* you *use to watch* the news on TV when you were little? News programmes ² _____ very different in the past. Women ³ _____ as newsreaders then, but now both men and women do the job. Newsreaders ⁴ _____ very smart in the past because they always wore suits. They were more serious than they are now, and they ⁵ _____ a lot. Today newsreaders are a lot friendlier, and they don't wear such formal clothes. The programmes are also more enjoyable now because they show reports from all over the world. This ⁶ _____ in early news programmes because there wasn't the technology to send images from one place to another. In the past, the same newsreader ⁷ _____ the same news stories several times a day. That was when families ⁸ _____ together to watch the news because they only had one television.

Vocabulary the news

4 Label the photo with the words in the box.

election flood forest fire ~~hurricane~~ robbery strike

1 hurricane
2 _____
3 _____
4 _____
5 _____
6 _____

5 Complete the words in the sentences.
1 You can read a_rticles_ in a newspaper or a magazine.
2 If you have a c_____, your car hits something and is damaged.
3 J_____ are people whose job it is to collect and write about news.
4 A n_____ d_____ is an event like a flood or a hurricane that causes a lot of damage.
5 If you r_____ a place, you arrive there.
6 If you r_____ something, you tell people exactly what you have seen or heard.
7 You can share information quickly and easily on the internet if you use s_____ m_____.
8 When things s_____, they affect a larger area or a bigger group of people.
9 If something is u_____ t_____ d_____, it has the most recent information.
10 If a magazine is published w_____, it appears every seven days.

6 Complete the article with the words in exercise **5**.

The power of nature

One of the worst **1** _natural disasters_ the world has ever seen was the 2011 tsunami. It was caused by a massive earthquake under the sea off the coast of Japan. In some areas, the water travelled up to 10 km from the coast, which made it difficult for rescue workers to **2** _____ the victims. **3** _____ flew to the area as soon as possible to **4** _____ on the damage, but before they got there, the news appeared on **5** _____. Once the story was on the internet, it quickly **6** _____ all over the world. For days after the event, there were **7** _____ in all the main newspapers explaining what was happening. The biggest danger came from a nuclear power plant called Fukushima which was in the area. Everybody wanted to be **8** _____ with the situation in the power plant. The **9** _____ magazines published photos of the tsunami that showed the power of the sea. The water picked up trees, buildings and cars and took them far away. In some places, the piles of vehicles looked like a big car **10** _____. It is estimated that around 19,000 people lost their lives in the tsunami.

I can ...	Very well	Quite well	More practice
talk about past habits and situations.	○	○	○
talk about the news.	○	○	○

11.3 Vocabulary development

Vocabulary — phrasal verbs

1 Rewrite the words in *italics* with the phrasal verbs in the box.

> find out   give up   grow up   put down   put on   set up   ~~take up~~

1 I've got more free time than I used to have, so I'm going to *start* a new sport.   *take up*
2 We called the station to *discover* the times of the trains.   _____
3 It was cold, so I *covered myself in* a warm coat before I left home.   _____
4 People often ask children what they want to be when they *get older*.   _____
5 They *placed* the new television carefully on the table.   _____
6 I couldn't do the homework so in the end, I had to *stop*.   _____
7 I know a lot about computers, but I can't afford to *start* my own company.   _____

2 Rewrite the sentences using a pronoun instead of a noun.

1 When did you find out your results?
   When did you find them out?
2 I'm giving up eating sweets.
   _____
3 He put down his suitcase on the platform.
   _____
4 When did you set up your home cinema system?
   _____
5 If you're cold, put your gloves on.
   _____
6 Why have you taken up yoga?
   _____

Vocabulary review

3 Complete the words and phrases related to global issues with the words in the box.

> economic   facts   farming   hunger   increasing   ~~technology~~   warming   wellbeing

Advances in science and [1] *technology*
The [2] _____ situation
[3] _____ and figures of the financial crisis
Food and [4] _____
Global [5] _____
Health and [6] _____
The [7] _____ population
World [8] _____

4 Complete the words and phrases related to the news with the missing vowels.

[1] *articles*   reach
  crash   [2] r_p_rt
[3] j_ _rn_l_sts   [4] s_c_ _l m_d_ _
[5] n_t_r_l d_s_st_rs   spread
  up to date   [6] w_ _kly

5 Complete the phrasal verbs with the particles in the box. You may use each particle more than once.

> down   on   out   up

1 carry *on* = continue
2 find _____ = discover
3 give _____ = stop
4 grow _____ = get older
5 put _____ = place
6 put _____ = cover something
7 set _____ = start something
8 take _____ = start a hobby

11.4 Speaking and writing

Speaking expressing and responding to opinions

1a Choose the correct option to complete the sentences.
A Beth, what do you think about all the security cameras on the streets today?
B Oh, I ¹ *take / think* we need them.
A Why's that?
B In my ² *point / view*, they help the police to catch criminals.
A I'm sorry, but I don't really ³ *agree / think*. It's very easy to break the cameras.
B ⁴ *Personally / True*, but what about the criminals who don't know that there's a camera?
A I take your ⁵ *opinion / point*, but the cameras make me feel like a criminal.
B That's ⁶ *OK / right*. It isn't very nice knowing that someone is watching you all the time.
A Exactly. ⁷ *Personally / True*, I don't like it at all.
B ⁸ *I'm sorry / Maybe*. Perhaps there shouldn't be so many of them.

b 11.4))) Listen and check.

2 Complete the conversations with the phrases in the box.

| a good point   ~~I agree~~   I disagree   I don't have |
| I don't think   In my opinion   Yeah, but |

1 A I don't think you should put your personal details on social media.
   B Yeah, _I agree_ .
2 A What do you think of modern technology?
   B _____, the world is changing too fast.
3 A I think people should pay to download films.
   B I'm afraid _____.
4 A Do you think people should stop posting photos on the internet?
   B Not really. _____ strong views on that.
5 A You should have a different password for each of your accounts.
   B _____ they're so difficult to remember.
6 A What's your opinion of free newspapers?
   B _____ you can believe everything you read.
7 A If you use a different name, your friends won't be able to find you.
   B That's _____.

Writing a presentation

3 Rewrite the sentences so that they are suitable for a slide.
1 You shouldn't tell friends your password.
   Never _tell friends your password._
2 No social network is 100% safe.
   Social _____
3 You shouldn't accept friend requests from strangers.
   Do _____
4 You should only chat with your real friends.
   Only _____
5 Don't post your holiday dates on Facebook.
   Do _____
6 You should always log off social media if you leave the room.
   Always _____

I can ...	Very well	Quite well	More practice
understand and use phrasal verbs.	○	○	○
express and respond to opinions.	○	○	○
give a presentation.	○	○	○

12 Work

12.1 The working environment

Vocabulary jobs, professions and workplaces

1 Complete the table with the words in the box.

building site ~~construction~~ hospital judge laboratory law medical research nurse office personal assistant

Job	Profession	Workplace
builder	1 *construction*	2 _____
3 _____	4 _____	court
5 _____	health care	6 _____
7 _____	administration	8 _____
scientist	9 _____	10 _____

2 Complete the puzzle with words for jobs, professions and the workplace.

¹D E V E L O P E R
² _ _ _ O _ _
³ _ _ _ L _
⁴ _ _ _ _ I _ _ _
⁵ _ _ _ _ T _ _
⁶ _ _ I _
⁷ _ _ _ C _
⁸S _ _ _ _ _

1 A software _____ is a person who designs computer programs.
2 A _____ is a building where goods are made by machines.
3 A _____ is a person who collects and writes about news.
4 _____ is the profession that builds machines and engines or roads and railways.
5 An _____ is a person who organizes a system or manages a business.
6 A _____ is a person who studies subjects like biology, chemistry or physics.
7 An _____ is a person who looks after the finances of a company.
8 _____ is the profession that deals with selling the products of a company.

3 Match the two halves of the sentences.
1 I'm an — a in health care.
2 I'm studying — b a personal assistant.
3 I work as — c accountant.
4 I work for — d law.
5 I work — e a construction company.
6 I'd like to — f become a software developer.

4 Complete the article with the words in the box.

accountant health care hospital laboratory medical nurse office ~~scientists~~

When people think about ¹*scientists*, they often imagine a person in a white coat doing experiments all day in a ² _____. In fact, modern scientists do a lot of different things during their working day, especially if they do ³ _____ research. Some of the researchers have their own ⁴ _____ with a desk and a computer where they can send and receive emails. They have to be in contact with other professionals so that they can share their ideas. Several times a week, they visit a ⁵ _____, where they can study some of the patients. Before they can go, they have to wait for a phone call from a ⁶ _____ who tells them the best time to visit. Of course, scientists need money to be able to do their research. If they work for a company, they have to talk to the ⁷ _____ before they can start a new project. The job of a scientist is very interesting, but it is also really important because they are trying to make ⁸ _____ better for everybody.

Grammar present perfect simple with *for* and *since*

5a Use the words to write present perfect simple sentences with *for* or *since*.

1 my father / have his car / too long
   My father has had his car for too long.
2 those children / study English / last year
   _____
3 my wife / like the same music / she was a student
   _____
4 my parents / be married / 30 years
   _____
5 John / work as a teacher / he left university
   _____
6 my friends / live in Scotland / six months
   _____

PRONUNCIATION *for* and *since*

b 12.1))) Listen and check your answers in exercise **5a**. Notice how *have* is pronounced /həv/ and *has* is pronounced /həz/ in the sentences.

c 12.1))) Listen again. Pause the CD and repeat after each sentence.

6 Use the words to write present perfect questions and answers with *for* or *since*. Use contractions where possible.

1 you / have your current job (seven years)
   A How long *have you had your current job?*
   B *I've had my current job for seven years.*
2 your sister / live abroad (three months)
   A How long _____
   B She _____
3 your parents / work in engineering (they were young)
   A How _____
   B They _____
4 you / know your best friend (ages)
   A _____
   B I _____
5 your partner / be a software developer (he left university)
   A _____
   B He _____
6 your daughter / play the guitar (last year)
   A _____
   B She _____

7 Complete the article with the present perfect of the verbs in the box with *for* or *since*.

| be | have | ~~love~~ | not speak | use | want |

One of the most famous scientists in the world is probably Stephen Hawking. Now in his seventies, the physicist is still fascinated by space and the universe. He [1] *has loved* science and the sky *since* he was a child and today he is famous for his research. Stephen Hawking can't work in an office or a laboratory because he is a very ill man. He [2] _____ his illness _____ most of his life, and it means that he can use his mind, but not his body. He isn't able to walk, and he [3] _____ a wheelchair _____ nearly 50 years now. In 1985, he had an important operation and lost his voice forever. He [4] _____ a word _____ the operation, and today he uses a computer program to communicate. Stephen Hawking has been married twice, but he got divorced both times. Now he [5] _____ single _____ about ten years and he spends a lot of time with his children. His daughter, Lucy, helps him write his books. The scientist [6] _____ to travel to space _____ he visited the Kennedy Space Centre in 2007, where he experienced zero gravity. He is hoping to become a space tourist, when the first space flight takes place.

I can ...

	Very well	Quite well	More practice
talk about jobs and professions.	○	○	○
use the present perfect simple with *for* and *since*.	○	○	○

81

12.2 The changing face of work

Vocabulary job responsibilities

1 Circle the verbs that don't go with the words in **bold**.
1 answer / do / talk on **the phone**
2 attend / organize / train **meetings**
3 answer / deal with / give **customer enquiries**
4 entertain / give / write **presentations**
5 employ / recruit / run **new staff**
6 advise / entertain / recruit **clients**
7 employ / type up / write **reports**
8 attend / manage / work in **a team**

2 Complete the words in the sentences.
1 How many people work in your t_eam_ ?
2 When was the last time your company recruited new st_____?
3 Who does most of the pa_____ in your office?
4 Where do you go when you have to entertain cl_____?
5 How many m_____ do you have to attend each week?
6 Who deals with customer e_____ in your company?
7 Do you get nervous before you give pr_____?
8 Who runs the day-to-day b_____ of your department?
9 How many e_____ do you receive each day?

3 Complete the article with the correct form of the verbs in the box.

| advise attend deal with give ~~recruit~~ talk on |
| work in write |

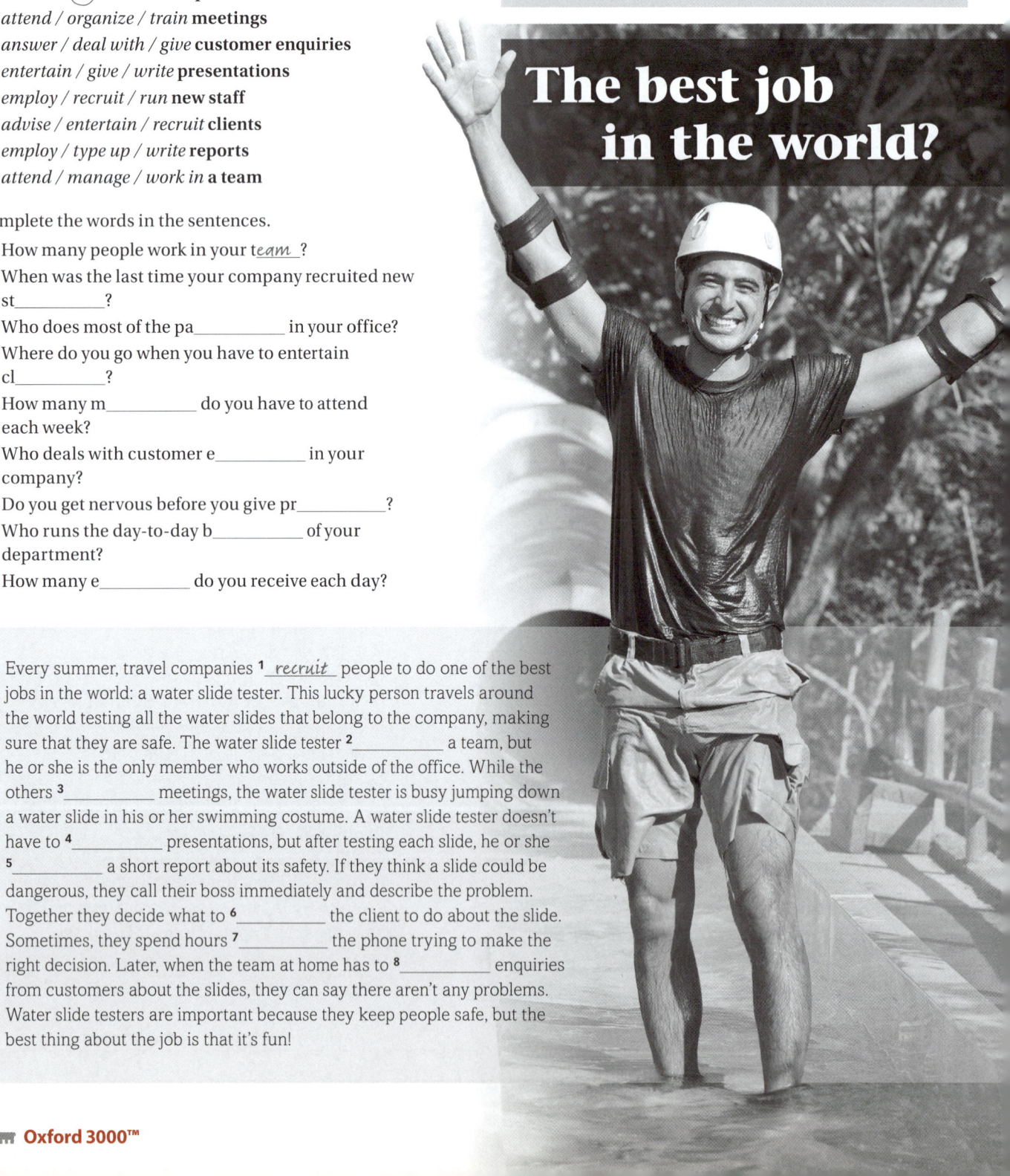

The best job in the world?

Every summer, travel companies **1** _recruit_ people to do one of the best jobs in the world: a water slide tester. This lucky person travels around the world testing all the water slides that belong to the company, making sure that they are safe. The water slide tester **2**_____ a team, but he or she is the only member who works outside of the office. While the others **3**_____ meetings, the water slide tester is busy jumping down a water slide in his or her swimming costume. A water slide tester doesn't have to **4**_____ presentations, but after testing each slide, he or she **5**_____ a short report about its safety. If they think a slide could be dangerous, they call their boss immediately and describe the problem. Together they decide what to **6**_____ the client to do about the slide. Sometimes, they spend hours **7**_____ the phone trying to make the right decision. Later, when the team at home has to **8**_____ enquiries from customers about the slides, they can say there aren't any problems. Water slide testers are important because they keep people safe, but the best thing about the job is that it's fun!

82 Oxford 3000™

Grammar uses of the infinitive with *to*

4 Match the two halves of the sentences.
1. Do some research before the interview — e
2. Leave home early and try — ___
3. If you're expecting a call, don't forget — ___
4. You don't need a pen because it isn't necessary — ___
5. Smile, although it's difficult — ___
6. Look smart on the day — ___

a not to feel nervous.
b to turn off your mobile phone.
c to take notes.
d to make a good impression.
e to find out about the company.
f not to be late.

5a Complete the sentences with the correct form of the verbs in brackets. Use the affirmative or negative form of the verbs.
1. I need _to work_ (work) late because I haven't finished my presentation for tomorrow.
2. Are you going to have a party _____ (celebrate) your birthday?
3. It's important _____ (say) the wrong thing to your boss.
4. I'll tell you if you promise _____ (tell) anybody.
5. Is it easy _____ (talk) to your colleagues outside work?
6. It's impossible _____ (worry) when your children come home late.
7. Remember _____ (call) me when I'm in the meeting.
8. Do you use your phone _____ (take) photos?

PRONUNCIATION *to* in infinitive with *to*

b 12.2))) Listen and check your answers to exercise **5a**. Pay attention to the weak pronunciation /tə/ of *to*.

c 12.2))) Listen again. Pause the CD and repeat after each sentence.

➡ **STUDY TIP** When an infinitive is used with *to*, the pronunciation of *to* is weak /tə/. Practise saying phrases with *to* and *not to* to get the pronunciation right.

6 Complete the article with the correct form of the verbs in the box.

| attend do get give go ~~have~~ open return |

More than words

Things often go wrong at job interviews and it is quite normal ¹ _to have_ a problem. The important thing is your reaction, which can sometimes get you the job. This is exactly what happened to an American woman who was invited ² _____ an interview at a company that was looking for a new receptionist. The woman parked outside the building, got out of her car and closed the door quickly … on her thumb! She needed the car keys ³ _____ the door, but they were in her bag. Eventually, she managed ⁴ _____ the keys and open the car door, but her thumb was hurting a lot. She decided ⁵ _____ to the interview anyway. She greeted the interviewer, and everything was going well until he asked her ⁶ _____ a typing test. She explained that she couldn't do the test because of her accident and she offered ⁷ _____ the next day. The interviewer got some ice for her thumb, and asked her a few more questions before she left. The next day she had a call from the company saying that they wanted ⁸ _____ her the job. She had been so calm after her accident that they thought she would make an excellent receptionist.

I can …	Very well	Quite well	More practice
talk about what a job involves.	○	○	○
use the infinitive with *to*.	○	○	○

83

12.3 Vocabulary development

Vocabulary: phrases with *in*

1 Replace the words in *italics* with a phrase with *in* and a word in the box.

| charge | common | ~~construction~~ | detail | hurry | mess |
| middle | suit | time | trouble |

1 You have to be very strong to work *as a builder*.
   in construction
2 My girlfriend and I get on so well because we have a lot *of the same interests*. _____
3 If you're late again, you'll be *asked to speak to the manager*. _____
4 Her brother is the man over there *wearing matching jacket and trousers*. _____
5 She's Head of Human Resources so she's *the person who controls* recruiting new staff. _____
6 I'm going to the bus stop because the bus leaves *five minutes from now*. _____
7 They're *driving very quickly* because they have to go to the airport. _____
8 I'm not surprised you can't find anything. Your room is *untidy* again. _____
9 He completely forgot what he was going to say *during* his speech. _____
10 First you need to make a plan, and then you can write it *with all the facts*. _____

Vocabulary review

2 Complete the table with the words in the box.

| ~~administrator~~ | court | engineering | hospital | judge | law |
| office | sales | scientist |

Jobs	Professions	Workplaces
accountant	administration	building site
¹ *administrator*	construction	7 _____
builder	4 _____	factory
journalist	health care	8 _____
2 _____	information technology (IT)	laboratory
nurse	5 _____	9 _____
personal assistant	medical research	
3 _____	politics	
software developer	6 _____	

3 Complete the words with the missing vowels.

Verbs	Nouns
advise / entertain	¹ cli*e*nts
answer / deal with	² _nqu_r__s
answer / talk on	³ th_ ph_n_
attend / organize	⁴ m__t_ngs
employ / recruit / train	⁵ st_ff
give / write	⁶ pr_s_nt_t__ns
manage / work in	a ⁷ t__m

4 Complete the missing vowels in the prepositional phrases with *in*.

fixed phrases
  in a mess, ¹ in d*e*t*ai*l, in trouble, ² _n c_mm_n, in charge of, in a hurry

talking about position or time
  ³ _n t_n m_n_t_s, in the distance, ⁴ _n th_ m_ddl_, in five years' time, in front of

talking about a profession
  ⁵ _n n_rs_ng, in education, ⁶ _n s_l_s

wearing something
  ⁷ _n _ s__t, dressed in black, ⁸ _n sh_rts

12.4 Speaking and writing

Writing a curriculum vitae (CV)

1 Match headings 1–8 to information a–h.

1 Nationality
2 Date of birth
3 Email address
4 Education and qualifications
5 Work experience
6 Skills
7 Interests
8 Referee

a Drama and Yoga
b Bachelor of Science in Computer Science
c Business intelligence. Fluent in English and Spanish.
d 11 May 1987
e Portuguese
f Josie@pmail.pt
g Paola da Santos, Compufield Lisbon
h 2008–present: Software developer, Compufield Lisbon.

2 Complete the extract from a CV.

Work experience

Technical Director, MH Communications
- ¹ m<u>anaged</u> a team of eight employees
- gave ² tr_____ in programming to new staff
- ³ dev_____ a customer service plan
- ⁴ att_____ courses about new models regularly
- prepared schedules and ⁵ pr_____ weekly reports
- ⁶ ass_____ the management in visiting clients

Skills
- ⁷ fl_____ in English, ⁸ b_____ French,
- good ⁹ kn_____ of most recent equipment

Referees
- on ¹⁰ re_____

Speaking answering questions in a job interview

3a Complete the interview with the phrases in the box.

> I can   I'd really like to get into   I find it hard to
> I'm currently working for   I'm good at
> ~~I've got a university degree in~~   I've worked as a

A Robert, what qualifications have you got for this job?
B Well, ¹ <u>I've got a university degree</u> in Sports Management.
A Oh good, and how much experience have you got?
B ² _____ sports centre manager for three years and ³ _____ Pinto Sports near Madrid.
A Right. So why do you want to work for this company?
B I'm enjoying my job right now, but ⁴ _____ community sports.
A Sure. And what are your strengths and weaknesses?
B Strengths? Well, ⁵ _____ dealing with the public, and ⁶ _____ work well in a team. As for weaknesses, ⁷ _____ switch off at the end of the day. But I'm working on that.

b 12.3))) Listen and check.

I can …	Very well	Quite well	More practice
understand and use phrases with *in*.	○	○	○
write a CV.	○	○	○
take part in a job interview.	○	○	○

85

12.5 Listening for pleasure

Easter Island statues

1. Look at the photo of a statue. Match the two halves of the sentences.

   1 The statue   a are found on Easter Island.
   2 Moais   b is in the South Pacific.
   3 Easter Island   c is called a moai.

2. 12.4))) Listen to a radio documentary about Easter Island and the Rapa Nui people.

3. 12.4))) Listen again. Choose the correct options to complete the summary.

   > There are **1** 787 / (887) moai on Easter Island. When the Rapa Nui arrived, there were a lot of **2** *statues / trees* on the island. At first life was **3** *easy / difficult* for the Rapa Nui, but everything changed when they started to **4** *make statues / build houses*. They needed wood for **5** *construction / transport*, but in the end, they used too much of it. The Rapa Nui people disappeared because they used all of the **6** *stone / trees* on Easter Island.

4. Think about the story of the Rapa Nui again. Did you find the story surprising. Why/Why not?

86

Review: Units 11 and 12

Grammar

1 Complete the sentences with the correct form of the verbs in the box.

arrive buy have look after phone stop

1 It's important _to arrive_ on time for a job interview.
2 If we _____ the environment, we wouldn't have as many problems.
3 People used to _____ their friends instead of using social media.
4 We _____ the same boss for many years.
5 Firefighters tried _____ the forest fire before it spread.
6 I _____ an electric car if they were cheaper.

2 Complete the text with one word in each space.

Would you visit Chernobyl ¹ _if_ you had the chance? If you went there today, you ² _____ find a very different city than the one that existed before. Chernobyl didn't ³ _____ to be famous until its nuclear power plant exploded in 1986. 14,000 people ⁴ _____ to live in the city, but they all had to leave after the accident. Chernobyl has been empty ⁵ _____ then, although about 500 residents ⁶ _____ recently returned to their homes. It isn't easy ⁷ _____ visit the area, because it is still very dangerous. There is a big fence with a lot of signs warning people ⁸ _____ to go any further. The only way to enter is on an official tour, but that can be quite expensive.

Vocabulary

3 Match definitions 1-6 to words and phrases in the box.

cure journalist judge reach recruit report

1 a person who writes articles for a newspaper _journalist_
2 arrive at a place _____
3 treatment that can make somebody healthy again _____
4 give people information about something that has happened _____
5 find new people for a job _____
6 a person who has to decide how to punish a criminal _____

4 Complete the words in the text.

The job market is not looking good these days, and it's pretty clear that ¹ u_nemployment_ is likely to rise in the future. ² A_____ in science and technology mean that machines and robots have taken many of the jobs that humans used to do. So which jobs are likely to exist and which will disappear? There may be less work in ³ c_____ soon because of new techniques in 3D printing. On the other hand, there will be more posts for ⁴ s_____ d_____, because computers will be more important in our lives. In ⁵ h_____ c_____, we will still need ⁶ n_____ to look after patients because this is something that machines can't do. But there will probably be fewer jobs in ⁷ a_____ because a new generation of office robots will do all the ⁸ p_____.

5 Choose the correct option to complete the sentences.

1 Why do children *grow up* / *set up* so quickly?
2 Who is *in the middle of* / *in charge of* recruiting new staff in your company?
3 How much do you have *in trouble* / *in common* with your colleagues?
4 How long do you think you will *put down* / *carry on* working before you can retire?
5 Do you keep your desk tidy or is it usually *in detail* / *in a mess*?
6 Where can I *find out* / *put on* more about global warming?

Speaking

6 Put the words in the correct order to make sentences.

1 sorry, / agree / I / but / don't / I'm / really
   I'm sorry, but I don't really agree.
2 currently / company / an / working / I'm / for / IT
   _____
3 really / sales / to / I'd / get / like / into
   _____
4 not / opinion, / exist / world / should / my / In / hunger
   _____
5 strong / have / media / the / views / don't / on / I
   _____
6 in / it / work / hard / I / team / find / to / a
   _____

87

Audioscripts

Unit 1 Time

Page 5, Exercises 4b & c

1.1

1
- A What time do you get up during the week?
- B At half past seven.

2
- A Who is the first person you see every morning?
- B My brother. He gets up at the same time as me.

3
- A Where do you have breakfast?
- B In the kitchen.

4
- A How much coffee do you drink?
- B I have three or four cups a day.

5
- A When do you stop for lunch?
- B From one o'clock until two.

6
- A How often do you eat in a restaurant?
- B About twice a month.

7
- A How many good friends do you have?
- B A lot. I have a lot of good friends.

8
- A What kind of car do you drive?
- B I drive a Mini.

Page 5, Exercises 5b & c

1.2

1 When is your birthday?
2 Who do you chat with online?
3 What kind of films do you like?
4 Are you busy right now?
5 How often do you spend time with relatives?
6 How many hours did you sleep last night?
7 Where are you from?
8 Did you go shopping yesterday?

Page 6, Exercises 1b & c

1.3

1 They often go out for a coffee.
2 My girlfriend goes running every now and then.
3 We don't usually go camping in the summer.
4 My best friend does aerobics once or twice a week.
5 I hardly ever play computer games.
6 My family don't often make future plans.

Page 9, Exercises 2b & c

1.4

1 I love going clubbing.
2 I can't stand the winter.
3 I'm really into yoga.
4 My favourite sport is basketball.
5 I don't mind doing housework.
6 I'm not keen on thunderstorms.
7 I quite like going camping.
8 I prefer football to golf.
9 I'm really interested in doing karate.

Unit 2 Inside outside

Page 10, Exercises 4b & c

2.1

1 cleaner
2 crowded
3 lively
4 market
5 pavement
6 pedestrian
7 performer
8 rubbish
9 souvenir
10 statue

Page 11, Exercises 5b & c

2.2

1 We're tired. We're having an early night.
2 My husband is late for work. He's running out of the door.
3 You can turn the TV off. I'm not watching it.
4 Your dog is hungry. It's waiting by the cupboard.
5 Can you help me? I'm doing my English homework.
6 My parents are angry. They aren't talking to each other.
7 Robert is in bed. He isn't feeling very well.
8 My grandfather is 80 today. We're celebrating his birthday with him.

Page 12, Exercises 4b & c

2.3

1 It's something that you have in your house.
2 It's something that you turn on and off.
3 It's something that has water in it.

Page 15, Exercise 1b

2.4

- A Please could you tell us how to get to the town hall?
- B Yes, go straight down here, cross the road at the lights and take the second left.
- A Can you show us on the map?
- B Yes, here it is. You can't miss it.
- A OK, so it's down here and second left after the lights?
- B That's right. It takes about ten minutes.
- A Thanks.

Unit 3 Going up, going down

Page 19, Exercises 5b & c

3.1

1 dived dropped jumped landed
2 booked climbed lifted walked
3 arrived travelled turned wanted
4 asked looked waited worked
5 called painted played listened
6 danced helped started watched

Page 20, Exercises 1c & d

3.2

One syllable:
calm, pleased, scared, stressed

Two syllables:
angry, anxious, confused, guilty, lonely, nervous

Three syllables:
embarrassed, excited, exhausted

Four syllables:
disappointed

Page 23, Exercise 1b

3.3

Conversation 1
- A We had a bad experience when we were on holiday a few years ago. We hired a car and went exploring on the coast.

88

A In the Canary Islands – in Fuerteventura, to be exact. So, anyway, we were in this hired car and we decided to leave the main road. We were driving in some sand when, suddenly, the car got stuck.
B Oh no!
A That's what I thought. I was so angry with my husband – he went right when I said left, and suddenly, we were lost and stuck.
B So, what did you do?
A We walked about five kilometres to the nearest road, and then we got a taxi back to our hotel, where we called for help. It was all OK in the end, but it cost us €250 to get the car out of the sand!

Conversation 2
A A funny thing happened last weekend when we went for a walk. We parked our car in a pretty little village and walked over the mountains to the next village. We were hoping to get a bus back to our car.
B So, what happened?
A We asked in a café about the buses, but there weren't any.
B You're joking!
A No, it's true. The café was full, so we left and started looking for a place to have lunch. We were walking along the road when a woman stopped her car and told us to get in.
B Why did she do that?
A She heard us ask about the buses in the café, so she knew where we wanted to go. You see, she was working in the village where our car was, and so she took us there on the way to work. We were so pleased!

Unit 4 Changes and challenges

Page 25, Exercises 6a & b
4.1))
1 When did you learn to drive?
2 What did you decide to wear?
3 Who did you want to win?
4 How much did you plan to spend?
5 Where would you like to go?
6 Why did you need to stop?

Page 26, Exercise 2b
4.2))
1
A What do you do when you're feeling lonely?
B I text friends. They always make me feel better.
2
A What's the first thing you do on Monday mornings?
B I deal with emails. I usually have hundreds to answer.
3
A Do you ever buy a newspaper?
B No, I read the news on the internet.
4
A Where do you pay your electricity bill?
B On the internet. I do online banking so I don't have to leave my house.
5
A How often do you use social media?
B A lot. But you don't need to update your Facebook page every day – you can add photos and comments when you like.
6
A How did you listen to that song?
B On my mobile phone. I often download music from the internet.
7
A Have you got a digital camera?
B No, I use my phone because it's easier to share photos with my friends.
8
A Are you worried about internet security?
B Not really. I never post personal information on a website.

Page 29, Exercises 1b & c
4.3))
A Are you doing anything at the weekend?
B I'm working on Saturday, but I'm free on Sunday.
A Do you fancy going to the Renoir exhibition at the Prado?
B Yeah, I'd love to.
A Shall we meet outside the museum when it opens?
B I'm afraid I can't go that early, because I'm playing tennis. Could we meet in the afternoon instead?
A Sure. Is two o'clock OK for you?
B Two o'clock is perfect. See you there.

Page 30, Exercises 2 & 3
4.4))
P = Presenter, A = Amy
P It takes a long time to build a house, and the end result is usually very expensive, as you know if you're trying to buy one. But a Chinese company has found a fantastic new way to make houses that are cheap AND take less time to build. Amy Chang is here to tell us all about them. Amy, how are the houses made?
A Well, believe it or not, they are made by a 3D computer printer.
P A computer printer! You're joking!
A No, I'm not. It's true. But this computer printer is no ordinary printer. It's absolutely huge. The printer is 150 metres long and ten metres wide. It doesn't print the finished house, but it prints the different parts of it. Then, workers have to put the parts together to make the house.
P But what is the house made of? It obviously isn't paper!
A No, no. The house is made of concrete. But the interesting thing is that the company is using recycled waste to make the concrete. The waste comes from building and industry and the company needs a lot of it to make the houses. That's why they're going to build a hundred new factories in China to recycle the waste.
P So the houses are green as well as cheap and easy to build. Amy, what does a printed house look like?
A Well, these houses are much smaller than normal ones and they only have one floor. But you can have a window if you want, and you can divide the house into two rooms. It depends on the design, really.
P And what about the price? How much does one of these printed houses cost?
A Each one costs around 3,650 euros. But you have to go to China to buy one. Actually, the houses aren't really for people like you and me. They are really for people without a home. Perhaps they are too poor to buy a house or maybe they have lost their home in a natural disaster. The company that makes them,

the WinSun Decoration Design Engineering Company, has spent years working on the houses – and the printer.
P Well, I think it's a great idea! Amy Chang, thank you for joining us.

Unit 5 Stuff and things

Page 32, Exercises 4b & c

5.1 🔊

1 useful	5 special
2 heavy	6 antique
3 leather	7 plastic
4 metal	8 tiny

Page 34, Exercises 1a & b

5.2 🔊
1 bag
2 note
3 bill
4 purse
5 credit card
6 wallet

Page 37, Exercise 1b

5.3 🔊
A Good morning. Are you looking for anything in particular?
B Oh, hello. Yes, I am, but I don't know the word in English.
A Well, can you describe it for me?
B Yes, it's a thing that you use to keep warm in the winter.
A Is it something you wear?
B No, it looks like a carpet, but it's smaller.
A And do you put it on the floor?
B That's right. Do you know what I mean?
A Yes, I do. It's a rug. Come with me and I'll show you where they are.

Unit 6 People

Page 38, Exercises 3b & c

6.1 🔊
1 clever honest lazy patient
2 confident sociable
3 creative untidy

Page 40, Exercises 4b & c

6.2 🔊
1 son mother adopt
2 aunt father parent
3 divorced cousin uncle
4 daughter engaged sister-in-law
5 couple husband only

Unit 7 Travel

Page 47, Exercises 5a & b

7.1 🔊
I might buy a car.
I might buy a car.

Page 47, Exercise 5c

7.2 🔊
1 I might go to Canada this year.
2 She might take you to the station.
3 You might get a seat.
4 It might rain later.
5 We might catch the train if we run.

Page 48, Exercises 4b & c

7.3 🔊
1 book your flight
2 lie by the pool
3 try the local food
4 hire a car
5 read a guidebook
6 apply for a visa
7 go sightseeing
8 explore the area

Page 51, Exercise 1b

7.4 🔊
A Hi, I'd like to check in, please.
B Yes, of course. Do you have a reservation?
A Yes, my name's Tatiana Genieva.
B OK, Ms Genieva. So that's a single room just for one night?
A Yeah, that's right.
B Could you fill in the registration form, please?
A Yeah, sure. Just one question. What time is check-out?
B You have to vacate your room by 10.30.
A Right. Is there anywhere I can leave my luggage tomorrow?
B Yes, you can leave it behind reception.
A Thanks a lot.

Unit 8 Language and learning

Page 52, Exercises 1b & c

8.1 🔊
1 My sister isn't able to walk because she has broken her leg.
2 Are you able to lend me some money to go to a concert?
3 I'm able to drive but I haven't got a car.
4 We're able to see the sea from the window of our room.
5 Is your boyfriend able to speak any foreign languages?
6 I'm tired because I'm not able to sleep at night.

Page 55, Exercises 4a & b

8.2 🔊
1 You can use the internet.
2 You can't take photos.
3 You can sit here.
4 You can't walk on the grass.
5 You can pay by credit card.
6 You can't play football here.

Page 57, Exercise 2b

8.3 🔊
A = Amara, R = Raz
A Raz? Where are you?
R Hi, Amara. I'm on my way.
A Pardon?
R I'm on my way.
A Sorry, it's too noisy in here. Are you on your way? The party started an hour ago.
R Amara, I'm nearly there. But I've forgotten your address.
A Sorry, Raz. You're breaking up. Can you remember my address?
R No, that's the problem.
A Raz, please could you speak up?
R OK. IS THAT BETTER?
A Yes, that's much better. I said can you remember my address? It's number 107.
R Could you repeat that, please?
A 1-0-7. A hundred and seven South View Avenue.
R Right. Please could you explain how to get there from the bus stop?
A OK. When you get off the bus, walk up the hill and take the second right.
R Amara, this is a really bad connection.
A Up the hill and second right. Did you get that?
R Sorry, I'm a bit lost …
A Raz. Raz? He's gone.

Page 58, Exercises 2 & 3

8.4 🔊
Speaker 1
This happened on a car journey we did one spring – to the village where my mother-in-law lives. We decided to drive over the mountains, but it started to snow, and soon there was ice and snow everywhere. We had to drive very slowly and there were a lot of cars at the side of the road. Fortunately, my husband is a very good driver, so we got there in the end.

Speaker 2
I had a very bad experience one night when I was riding home on my bike. I had my lights on and everything, but that didn't seem to make any difference. I came to a roundabout where I wanted to go straight on, but suddenly this lorry appeared. It crossed over right in front of me – it was so close that it touched my foot. I don't know how I didn't fall off my bike!

Speaker 3
I was in a hotel once and I couldn't sleep. I got up to look out of the window, and I saw some big black clouds in the sky. Only they weren't clouds, and I suddenly realized that there was a fire – in my hotel! I didn't know what to do. Luckily, the emergency services were already there, and somebody came to take me outside. What a nightmare!

Speaker 4
I've never been very keen on flying, but my last trip was worse than ever. The weather was awful, and it was really cloudy, so the pilot was having problems landing. The plane was moving all over the place, and everybody was holding on to their seats. We tried to land three times before we actually stopped going up in the air again. It was very frightening, I can tell you.

Speaker 5
I had a really frightening experience on a train once. A man got on the train and sat down opposite me. We got talking, and to start with, he seemed really nice. Then he told me to give him my mobile phone. Of course, I said no, but then he started shouting at me and I was really frightened because there weren't many people around. I gave him my phone in the end, and he got off at the next station with it.

Speaker 6
My most frightening experience was when I nearly drowned. I was swimming in the sea off the coast of Mauritius about four years ago and suddenly I couldn't stand in the water and the sea was moving me away from my friends and I couldn't get back to them. One friend saw what was happening and said, 'Don't panic! Just wait until the current brings you back!' And luckily it did. But I never went in the sea again on that holiday!

Speaker 7
I was very frightened about six weeks ago when my six-year-old son had problems while he was eating dinner. He had been eating steak and put a large piece into his mouth and then tried to eat it but it was stuck and he couldn't breathe! His face became red and he didn't know what to do and neither did I. Fortunately my sister was in the house and she hit him on the back, then the piece of meat came out. But we were all very frightened and we cried a lot.

Unit 9 Body and mind

Page 61, Exercises 6a & b

9.1
1 I'll
2 You'll
3 It'll
4 He'll
5 She'll
6 We'll
7 They'll

Page 62, Exercises 4b & c

9.2
1 eat   read
2 bread   meat
3 disease   dream
4 easy   weather
5 health   leather
6 already   instead
7 breakfast   team
8 cleaner   pleased

Page 65, Exercise 2b

9.3
A Morning. How can I help you?
B Hello. Have you got anything for a cold?
A Well, there isn't much I can do really. I think you should go home and get lots of rest.
B Can you give me something for my cough? It's very annoying.
A Yes, you could try this medicine. Take it every six hours until the cough goes away.
B Right.
A It's a good idea to drink lots of water, too. And keep warm. You mustn't go out.
B OK. Thank you very much.

Unit 10 Food

Page 67, Exercises 4b & c

10.1
Two-syllable words:
chocolate
different
favourite
raspberry
restaurant
several
strawberry

Three-syllable words:
interesting
temperature
vegetable

Page 68, Exercises 2b & c

10.2
four tins of chicken soup
six packets of sausages
two bottles of ketchup
two tubes of tomato paste
three jars of olives
two boxes of strawberries
four cartons of cream
sixteen cans of drinks

Page 71, Exercise 2b

10.3
Conversation 1
A Excuse me? I'm afraid I can't eat this steak. It's raw.
B Really? I'll take it back to the kitchen for you.
A No, I'd like to order something else, please.
B Of course. What would you like?
A I'm not sure. Would you mind bringing me the menu again?
B Of course not. I'm terribly sorry about your steak.
A Don't worry about it. Erm, I'll have a salad, please.

Conversation 2
A Excuse me? Could you possibly bring me the bill?
B Yes, of course … Here it is.
A Oh. There seems to be a mistake.
B Is there?
A Yes. You've charged me for the steak, but I didn't eat it.
B You're absolutely right. I do apologize.
A Don't worry. It's not your fault.

Unit 11 World

Page 75, Exercise 4b
11.1
1 If I had a car, I would drive to work.

Page 75, Exercises 4c & d
11.2
2 I wouldn't be happy if I lost my job.
3 What would you do if you could go back in time?
4 If she knew his number, she'd call him.
5 Where would you live if you had the choice?
6 You'd feel better if you did some exercise.

Page 76, Exercise 1b & d
11.3
1 My brother used to work in a bank.
2 We didn't use to have a garden.
3 My parents used to live in a flat.
4 Did you use to have long hair?
5 I didn't use to drink coffee.
6 Did your boyfriend use to have a motorbike?
7 I used to wear glasses.

Page 79, Exercise 1b
11.4
A Beth, what do you think about all the security cameras on the streets today?
B Oh, I think we need them.
A Why's that?
B In my view, they help the police to catch criminals.
A I'm sorry, but I don't really agree. It's very easy to break the cameras.
B True, but what about the criminals who don't know that there's a camera?
A I take your point, but the cameras make me feel like a criminal.
B That's right. It isn't very nice knowing that someone is watching you all the time.
A Exactly. Personally, I don't like it at all.
B Maybe. Perhaps there shouldn't be so many of them.

Unit 12 Work

Page 81, Exercises 5b & c
12.1
1 My father has had his car for too long.
2 Those children have studied English since last year.
3 My wife has liked the same music since she was a student.
4 My parents have been married for 30 years.
5 John has worked as a teacher since he left university.
6 My friends have lived in Scotland for six months.

Page 83, Exercises 5b & c
12.2
1 I need to work late because I haven't finished my presentation for tomorrow.
2 Are you going to have a party to celebrate your birthday?
3 It's important not to say the wrong thing to your boss.
4 I'll tell you if you promise not to tell anybody.
5 Is it easy to talk to your colleagues outside work?
6 It's impossible not to worry when your children come home late.
7 Remember not to call me when I'm in the meeting.
8 Do you use your phone to take photos?

Page 85, Exercise 3b
12.3
A Robert, what qualifications have you got for this job?
B Well, I've got a university degree in Sports Management.
A Oh good, and how much experience have you got?
B I've worked as a sports centre manager for three years and I'm currently working for Pinto Sports near Madrid.
A Right. So why do you want to work for this company?
B I'm enjoying my job right now, but I'd really like to get into community sports.
A Sure. And what are your strengths and weaknesses?
B Strengths? Well, I'm good at dealing with the public, and I can work well in a team. As for weaknesses, I find it hard to switch off at the end of the day. But I'm working on that.

Page 86, Exercises 2 & 3
12.4
Presenter: There is an island in the South Pacific, about 3,600 km from the coast of Chile, called Easter Island. It isn't huge, and it doesn't have any tall trees, but it has a lot of massive stone statues on it called *moai*. Most of the moai are over nine metres tall, and there are 887 of them in total. They were created between the years 1250 and 1500 by the people who lived there: the Rapa Nui.

The Rapa Nui arrived at Easter Island from across the sea in large wooden boats. At the time, the island was covered with very tall trees, and it was the perfect place to live. They used the wood from the trees to build houses and new boats to go fishing. There was more than enough food for everybody and the population grew. Soon, some people went to live in different parts of the island. Then, the Rapa Nui started to make statues. Nobody is sure of the reason for these statues, but some people say that one was made each time an important leader died. The statues were all made in the same place, and then they were transported across the island. Trees were cut down to transport the statues, and as more statues were made, more trees were cut down. In the end, the Rapa Nui cut down all of the trees on the island. This was a disaster. Now, there were no trees to protect the land, so they could not grow any plants, and they had no wood to make boats to go fishing. Soon, there was not enough food for everybody. People started fighting, and the Rapa Nui began to die of hunger. The population fell from 15,000 to around 750. It was the beginning of the end of the Rapa Nui.

Today, the only thing that remains of the Rapa Nui on Easter Island is the moai. But their story can teach us a valuable lesson. On such a small island, it was easy to see what was happening as the trees disappeared. But the people carried on cutting them down. The rest of us can learn from the Rapa Nui. We have already seen the natural disasters that happen when we don't look after the planet. But there is still time to save it. If we start taking more interest in the environment, the same thing that happened to the Rapa Nui may not happen to us.

Answer key

Unit 1 Time
1.1 Do you live in the past, present or future? page 4
Vocabulary daily life

1
1 g   5 h
2 d   6 a
3 f   7 c
4 b   8 e

2
1 *do*   6 have
2 do   7 have
3 do   8 make
4 have   9 do
5 go   10 have

3
1 *Eat healthy food*
2 go shopping
3 Do some exercise
4 stay in
5 Have an early night
6 go to bed late
7 Spend time with relatives
8 have a good time

Grammar question forms

4a
1 *What time*
2 Who
3 Where
4 How much
5 When
6 How often
7 How many
8 What kind

5a
1 *When is your birthday?*
2 Who do you chat with online?
3 What kind of films do you like?
4 Are you busy right now?
5 How often do you spend time with relatives?
6 How many hours did you sleep last night?
7 Where are you from?
8 Did you go shopping yesterday?

6
1 *Are you*
2 Did you have
3 When did you start
4 Are you
5 many did you win
6 do you live

7 How did you get
8 Do you want

1.2 Free time page 6
Grammar present simple & adverbs of frequency

1a
1 *They often go out for a coffee.*
2 My girlfriend goes running every now and then.
3 We don't usually go camping in the summer.
4 My best friend does aerobics once or twice a week.
5 I hardly ever play computer games.
6 My family don't often make future plans.

2
1 *always does exercise*
2 rarely have a lie-in
3 Most days my sister goes on Facebook
4 go on holiday once or twice a year
5 Every now and then we go clubbing

3
1 *hardly ever have*
2 is never
3 always eat healthily
4 nearly always go
5 sometimes watch videos
6 occasionally spend time with relatives
7 often chat with friends online
8 are usually

Vocabulary free-time activities

4
1 *play basketball*
2 go on Facebook
3 go clubbing
4 do aerobics
5 go to the gym
6 play cards
7 do yoga
8 go camping

5
1 *aerobics*
2 swimming
3 golf
4 basketball
5 karate
6 exercise

6
1 *play computer games*
2 go swimming
3 do exercise
4 play golf
5 go for a walk
6 go running
7 play football
8 go for a meal

1.3 Vocabulary development page 8
Vocabulary nouns and verbs with the same form

1
1 *photographs, photograph*
2 experience, experience
3 plan, plan
4 dream, dream
5 text, text
6 promise, promise
7 posts, post

2
1 *texts*
2 photographs
3 plan
4 experience
5 photograph
6 post
7 dream

Vocabulary review

3
chat: chat with friends online
do: do homework, do housework, do some exercise, do some work, do the shopping
eat: eat healthy food
go: go on a trip, go shopping, go to bed late
have: *have a family meal*, have a good time, have a lie-in, have an early night, have fun
make: make a to-do list, make future plans
spend: spend time with relatives
stay: stay in

4
1 go
2 play
3 do

5
1 have
2 take
3 make

94

ANSWER KEY

1.4 Speaking and writing page 9
Speaking talking about the weather

1   1 *damp*   4 humid
   2 showers   5 thunderstorm
   3 pleasant   6 mild

Speaking talking about likes and dislikes

2a 1 *love going clubbing.*
    2 I can't stand the winter.
    3 I'm really into yoga.
    4 My favourite sport is basketball.
    5 I don't mind doing housework.
    6 I'm not keen on thunderstorms.
    7 I quite like going camping.
    8 I prefer football to golf.
    9 I'm really interested in doing karate.

Writing a web post about the best time to visit your country

3   1 *but*   4 and
   2 but   5 So
   3 and   6 and

Unit 2 Inside outside
2.1 Street life page 10
Vocabulary street life

1   1 *huge*   4 safe
   2 crowded   5 dirty
   3 lively   6 dull

2   1 *street cleaner*
   2 pedestrian area
   3 souvenir seller
   4 market place
   5 pavement artist
   6 parking space
   7 street performer

3   1 *lively*
   2 pedestrian area
   3 market place
   4 stalls
   5 street performers
   6 souvenir sellers
   7 huge
   8 crowded
   9 safe
   10 dirty
   11 rubbish
   12 street cleaners

4a 1 *cleaner*
    2 crowded
    3 lively
    4 market
    5 pavement
    6 pedestrian
    7 performer
    8 rubbish
    9 souvenir
    10 statue

Grammar present simple and present continuous

5a 1 *'re having*
    2 's running
    3 'm not watching
    4 's waiting
    5 'm doing
    6 aren't talking
    7 isn't feeling
    8 're celebrating

6   1 *are you going*, Do you want
   2 Are you listening, like
   3 do you do, go
   4 does the market open, don't know
   5 Is your partner, doesn't work
   6 Are you having, 'm having
   7 Do I need, isn't raining
   8 Is our team winning, 're playing

7   1 *I never make a to-do list.*
   2 My parents have a family meal every Sunday.
   3 We're eating healthy food these days.
   4 My partner is doing some work at the moment.
   5 Luca always goes to bed late.
   6 I'm chatting with friends online right now.

8   1 *starts*
   2 finishes
   3 has
   4 gets
   5 are sitting
   6 are watching
   7 is buying
   8 is looking
   9 wants
   10 like
   11 is becoming
   12 are spending

2.2 Home life page 12
Grammar identifying relative clauses

1   1 *that*   4 that
   2 where   5 who
   3 where   6 which

2a 1 *who, neighbour*
    2 where, garage
    3 which, picture
    4 which, DVD
    5 who, dentist
    6 which, ball
    7 where, kitchen
    8 who, police officer

2b In sentences 1, 3, 4, 5, 6 and 8.

3   1 *which I wear to go running.*
   2 which I use for work.
   3 who repairs my car.
   4 where my grandfather always sits.
   5 who cuts my hair.
   6 which goes to the city centre.
   7 where we do our shopping.

4a 1 It's something that you have in your house.
    2 It's something that you turn on and off.
    3 It's something that has water in it.

Vocabulary household objects

5   1 *dishwasher*
   2 dustpan and brush
   3 wash basin
   4 microwave oven
   5 Satellite TV
   6 chest of drawers

6   1 *carpet*   5 towel
   2 mirror   6 cloth
   3 cooker   7 wardrobe
   4 sheet   8 duvet

7   1 *mirror*
   2 carpet
   3 towel
   4 wardrobe
   5 dustpan and brush
   6 dishwasher

2.3 Vocabulary development page 14

Vocabulary phrases with *on*

1   1 *on the internet*
    2 on the way
    3 on the left
    4 on holiday
    5 on TV
    6 on time
    7 on public transport
    8 on business

2   1 *on the way*
    2 on business
    3 on the left
    4 on public transport
    5 on holiday

Vocabulary review

3   1 *crowded*
    2 safe
    3 pavement artist
    4 street performer
    5 market place
    6 statue

4   1 *things in the bedroom*
    2 things in the kitchen
    3 things in the bathroom
    4 things in the sitting room
    5 things to clean with
    6 things to light when it gets dark

5   1 *checking news and information on the computer*
    2 on business
    3 positioned on the right-hand side
    4 on the way

2.4 Speaking and writing page 15

Speaking asking for and giving directions

1a 1 *Please could you tell us how to get to the town hall?*
    2 Yes, go straight down here, cross the road at the lights and take the second left.
    3 Can you show us on the map?
    4 Yes, here it is. You can't miss it.
    5 OK, so it's down here and second left after the lights?
    6 That's right. It takes about ten minutes.
    7 Thanks.

2   1 *'m looking*
    2 on
    3 far
    4 walk
    5 turn
    6 stairs
    7 see
    8 it's

3   1 *is this the right way*
    2 until you reach
    3 through the doors
    4 the first right
    5 I need to go
    6 that right
    7 on the left
    8 a lot

Writing text messages

4   1 *RU*   6 asap
    2 CU   7 Pls
    3 Rx   8 U
    4 Gr8   9 Thnx
    5 Sry

2.5 Reading for pleasure page 16

Pollution

1   water pollution

3   1 John does experiments to find out the effects of the waste products on rats and writes a report.
    2 David Wilson reads the report.
    3 John arrives in David Wilson's office.
    4 Wilson says he doesn't like the conclusions in the report.
    5 Wilson says he doesn't want to build new machines to clean up the waste products.
    6 John gets very nervous and drinks water.
    7 John says he's worried about the effects of the waste products.

Review: Units 1 and 2 page 17

Grammar

1   1 *who*
    2 once
    3 kind
    4 at
    5 every
    6 often

2   1 *Are you making*
    2 want
    3 leaves
    4 don't arrive

    5 lasts
    6 are offering
    7 are doing
    8 are looking

Vocabulary

3   1 *towel*
    2 have a lie in
    3 stall
    4 do aerobics
    5 dishwasher
    6 lively
    7 do housework
    8 go out for a meal

4   1 *huge*   5 chess
    2 crowded   6 chat
    3 stay   7 early
    4 rug

5   1 *on holiday*
    2 on public transport
    3 have a dream
    4 make a promise
    5 on time
    6 take a photograph

Speaking

6   1 *I prefer*
    2 Go straight down
    3 it's five minutes' walk
    4 I'm really

Unit 3 Going up, going down
3.1 The man who fell to Earth page 18

Vocabulary movement

1   1 *fall*   6 drop
    2 rise   7 lift
    3 land   8 dive
    4 take off   9 jump
    5 climb

2   1 *over*   5 through
    2 towards   6 backwards
    3 out of   7 round and round
    4 into   8 along

3   1 *into*   5 out of
    2 along   6 backwards
    3 through   7 over
    4 forward   8 towards

Grammar past simple

4   1 *The plane from Madrid landed at 22.40 last night.*
    2 The sun rose two hours ago.
    3 Did you go on holiday in the summer?

ANSWER KEY

4 We had a family meal the day before yesterday.
5 I didn't climb trees when I was young.
6 My friends went clubbing three days ago.
7 Did you spend time with relatives the other day?
8 We didn't do housework on / last Tuesday.

5a 1 *landed*
2 lifted
3 wanted
4 waited
5 painted
6 started

6 1 *became*
2 took off
3 flew
4 parachuted
5 didn't land
6 finished
7 saw
8 were
9 returned
10 didn't retire
11 travelled
12 worked
13 helped
14 crashed
15 died

3.2 Going up … One man's lift nightmare page 20

Vocabulary adjectives for describing feelings

1a 1 *excited*
2 angry
3 embarrassed
4 guilty
5 nervous
6 disappointed
7 confused
8 calm
9 lonely
10 anxious
11 pleased

1b One syllable: calm, pleased, scared, stressed
Two syllables: <u>ang</u>ry, <u>anx</u>ious, con<u>fused</u>, <u>guil</u>ty, <u>lone</u>ly, <u>ner</u>vous
Three syllables: embarrassed, ex<u>cit</u>ed, ex<u>haus</u>ted
Four syllables: disap<u>poin</u>ted

2b The missing feeling is 'in a good mood'

Grammar past simple and past continuous

3 1 *was raining*
2 were sleeping
3 wasn't working
4 were, talking
5 was driving
6 weren't watching
7 was living
8 were dancing

4 1 *I dropped a glass when I was doing the washing up.*
2 We were studying in the library when the fire started.
3 My partner broke his leg when he was playing football.
4 A thief took my bag when I was sitting in the park.
5 You were coming out of the supermarket when I saw you.
6 My friends were waiting outside the cinema when I arrived.

5 1 *saw*   6 was sitting
2 was doing   7 filled
3 thought   8 rose
4 didn't try 9 was going
5 asked   10 came

3.3 Vocabulary development page 22

Vocabulary adverbs of manner

1 1 *They play tennis badly.*
2 He reads slowly.
3 We eat healthily.
4 My mother walks fast.
5 I drive carefully.
6 You cook well.
7 My partner works hard.
8 My brother dresses smartly.

2 1 *regularly*
2 quietly
3 easily
4 beautifully
5 fluently
6 quickly
7 politely

Vocabulary review

3 1 going up
2 going down

4 1 *excited*   4 embarrassed
2 anxious   5 lonely
3 pleased   6 scared

5 1 *angrily*   4 fast
2 nice   5 politely
3 easily

3.4 Speaking and writing page 23

Speaking telling and responding to a story

1a 1 *We had a bad experience*
2 anyway
3 Oh no
4 I was so angry
5 It was all OK in the end
6 A funny thing happened
7 what happened
8 You're joking
9 We were so pleased

Writing email (1): describing an event

2 1 *a short time later*
2 when
3 Suddenly
4 At first
5 but then
6 In the end

Unit 4 Changes and challenges
4.1 Changing directions page 24

Vocabulary life stages and events

1 1 *in my mid-twenties*
2 middle-aged
3 in her early twenties
4 elderly
5 in her late twenties
6 in her sixties
7 about thirty-five
8 a child
9 a teenager.

2 1 d   5 g
2 e   6 f
3 a   7 h
4 c   8 b

3 1 *start*   4 have
2 choose   5 get
3 go to   6 leave

4 1 *took up*   5 started
2 left   6 got
3 decided   7 had
4 went   8 retired

97

Grammar verbs with -ing and to

5   1 *When did you learn to drive?*
    2 What did you decide to wear?
    3 Who did you want to win?
    4 How much did you plan to spend?
    5 Where would you like to go?
    6 Why did you need to stop?

7   1 *to play*   5 going
    2 living   6 to move
    3 to retire   7 doing
    4 playing   8 raining

8   1 *working*   6 to be
    2 to do   7 getting up
    3 to think   8 going
    4 to apply   9 to leave
    5 to look for   10 asking

4.2 Living without the internet
page 26

Vocabulary internet activities

1   1 *go online*
    2 do research
    3 blog
    4 chat online
    5 tweet
    6 shop online
    7 log on
    8 use social media

2a 1 *text friends*
    2 deal with emails
    3 read the news
    4 do online banking
    5 update your Facebook page
    6 download music
    7 share photos
    8 post personal information on a website

3   1 *use*   5 post
    2 go   6 read
    3 log on   7 tweet
    4 share   8 chat

Grammar going to and present continuous for the future

4   1 *He's going to jump.*
    2 They're going to do the shopping.
    3 She's going to have a baby.
    4 He's going to get married.
    5 They're going to play tennis.
    6 It's going to take off.

5   1 *going to check*
    2 going to update
    3 are coming
    4 having
    5 is going to land
    6 working

6   1 *I'm going to be*
    2 Are you having
    3 I'm going to take
    4 We're visiting
    5 I'm not working
    6 we're flying
    7 we're coming
    8 are you going to do
    9 We're going to go up
    10 we're going to see

4.3 Vocabulary development
page 28

Vocabulary get

1   1 *get married*
    2 get some shoes
    3 get a phone call
    4 get home
    5 get a job
    6 get some pizzas
    7 get bored
    8 get cold

2   1 *you get a new one?*
    2 get a job?
    3 get ready?
    4 get any presents?
    5 get a taxi?
    6 get home earlier?

Vocabulary review

3a 1 *about*   6 go to
    2 sixties   7 have
    3 career   8 -aged
    4 married   9 partner
    5 in   10 abroad

3b Numbers 1, 2, 5 and 8 are life stages; numbers 3, 4, 6, 7, 9 and 10 are life events.

4   1 *d*   7 a
    2 g   8 c
    3 j   9 f
    4 e   10 h
    5 k   11 b
    6 i

5   1 receive
    2 buy
    3 become

4.4 Speaking and writing page 29

Speaking inviting and making arrangements

1   1 *Are you doing anything at the weekend?*
    2 I'm working on Saturday, but I'm free on Sunday.
    3 Do you fancy going to the Renoir exhibition at the Prado?
    4 Yeah, I'd love to.
    5 Shall we meet outside the museum when it opens?
    6 I'm afraid I can't go that early, because I'm playing tennis. Could we meet in the afternoon instead?
    7 Sure. Is two o'clock OK for you?
    8 Two o'clock is perfect. See you there.

2   1 *Are you free*
    2 Would you like
    3 I can't make it
    4 How about
    5 be great
    6 We could try
    7 I'd like
    8 any good
    9 Sounds perfect

Writing email (2): making arrangements

3   1 *Hi there!*
    2 How are you doing?
    3 I'm really sorry but
    4 how about going out
    5 I'd love to
    6 Is that OK for you?
    7 Speak soon
    8 Love

4.5 Listening for pleasure page 30

Ecological housing

1   1 bricks   4 plastic/metal/wood
    2 *concrete*   5 plastic/wood/metal
    3 plastic/metal   6 glass

3   1 *printer*   5 100
    2 150   6 small
    3 parts   7 floor
    4 waste   8 3,650

ANSWER KEY

Review: Units 3 and 4 page 31

Grammar

1.
   1. going
   2. to retire
   3. to start
   4. changing
   5. to move
   6. playing
   7. to come
   8. failing

2.
   1. are your parents going to do
   2. they're going to relax
   3. They aren't going to stay
   4. is your dad going to do
   5. He's going to learn
   6. my mum is going to take up

3.
   1. moved
   2. didn't make
   3. was doing
   4. appeared
   5. became
   6. were watching
   7. didn't feel
   8. was lying

Vocabulary

4.
   1. pleased
   2. dive
   3. lonely
   4. drop
   5. guilty
   6. land

5.
   1. leave
   2. go
   3. retire
   4. log on
   5. deal with
   6. text
   7. do
   8. get

Speaking

6.
   1. are you free
   2. Do you fancy
   3. I'd love to
   4. How about
   5. I had a bad experience
   6. What happened?
   7. You're joking
   8. shall we

Unit 5 Stuff and things

5.1 Your world in objects page 32

Vocabulary adjectives for describing objects

1.
   1. metal
   2. useful
   3. comfortable
   4. thin
   5. gold
   6. special

2.
   1. gold
   2. light
   3. amazing
   4. leather
   5. special
   6. useful
   7. valuable
   8. ordinary

3.
   1. amazing
   2. heavy
   3. antique
   4. tiny
   5. brand new
   6. thin
   7. large
   8. comfortable

4. 'antique' has the stress on the second syllable because it's a foreign word (most English two-syllable words have stress on the first syllable).

Grammar articles

5.
   1. a
   2. the
   3. the
   4. ✗
   5. an
   6. The
   7. ✗
   8. a

6.
   1. ✓
   2. ✗ the planets
   3. ✗ a time capsule
   4. ✓
   5. ✗ life
   6. ✓
   7. ✗ music
   8. ✗ birds
   9. ✓
   10. ✗ the pictures
   11. ✗ the music
   12. ✓

7.
   1. the, the
   2. a, a
   3. a, ✗
   4. a, ✗
   5. ✗, the
   6. the, the

5.2 It's all about the money page 34

Vocabulary money

1a and c
   1. bag c
   2. note d
   3. bill e
   4. purse b
   5. credit card f
   6. wallet a

2.
   1. cash
   2. change
   3. bank account
   4. in debt
   5. amount
   6. balance
   7. rent

3.
   1. owe
   2. afford
   3. save up
   4. spend
   5. borrows
   6. pay for
   7. lends

Grammar quantifiers

4.
   1. some
   2. a lot of
   3. much
   4. few
   5. many
   6. any
   7. much
   8. enough

5.
   1. some
   2. any
   3. a few
   4. much
   5. enough
   6. lots of
   7. too much
   8. many

6.
   1. a few days
   2. too much shopping
   3. a little Portuguese
   4. some friends
   5. too many biscuits
   6. lots of things
   7. any petrol
   8. enough food

5.3 Vocabulary development page 36

Vocabulary suffixes

1.
   1. digital
   2. arrangements
   3. enjoyable
   4. buyer
   5. stressful
   6. normal
   7. equipment
   8. disappointment
   9. comfortable
   10. information

2.
   1. decision
   2. possessions
   3. essential
   4. useful
   5. beautiful
   6. fashionable
   7. suitable
   8. computers

Vocabulary review

3.
   1. colour
   2. opinion
   3. weight
   4. material
   5. age
   6. size / shape

4.
   1. balance
   2. cash
   3. note
   4. rent
   5. afford
   6. lend
   7. pay for
   8. save up

5.
   1. disappointment
   2. information
   3. buyer
   4. useful
   5. suitable
   6. normal

99

5.4 Speaking and writing page 37

Speaking explaining words you don't know

1a 1 *Good morning. Are you looking for anything in particular?*
    2 Oh hello. Yes, I am, but I don't know the word in English.
    3 Well, can you describe it for me?
    4 Yes, it's a thing that you use to keep warm in the winter.
    5 Is it something you wear?
    6 No, it looks like a carpet, but it's smaller.
    7 And do you put it on the floor?
    8 That's right. Do you know what I mean?
    9 Yes, I do. It's a rug. Come with me and I'll show you where they are.

2 1 *what's it called?*
   2 I've forgotten the word in English.
   3 It's quite big, like a sheet.
   4 You use it to dry yourself
   5 Exactly! That's what I'm looking for.

Writing email (3): returning an online product

1 *recently ordered*
2 I'm afraid I'm not happy
3 they are completely different
4 I didn't receive
5 I'd like to return
6 Could you please send
7 get a refund
8 Yours sincerely

Unit 6 People

6.1 The quiet revolution page 38

Vocabulary adjectives for describing character

1 1 *sociable*   5 untidy
   2 smart   6 confident
   3 quiet   7 clever
   4 lazy   8 honest

2 1 *clever*
   2 shy
   3 patient
   4 unsociable
   5 stupid
   6 hard-working
   7 tidy
   8 creative

3a Oo: *clever*, honest, lazy, patient
    Ooo: confident, sociable
    oOo: creative, untidy

Grammar making comparisons

4 1 *worse*, worst
   2 better, best
   3 more honest, most honest
   4 lazier, laziest
   5 older, oldest
   6 smarter, smartest
   7 more sociable, most sociable
   8 tidier, tidiest

5 1 *Fruit is healthier than chocolate.*
   2 Rugs are smaller than carpets.
   3 Monday is the worst day of the week.
   4 Gold is more expensive than plastic.
   5 I think skiing is the most exciting sport.
   6 They say flying is the safest way to travel.
   7 Your English is better than mine.
   8 My hometown is the liveliest place I know.

6 1 *isn't as difficult as Chinese.*
   2 isn't as wet as yesterday.
   3 isn't as thin as a sheet.
   4 isn't as hard-working as me.
   5 isn't as dark as mine.
   6 not as old as my wife.
   7 isn't as big as yours.
   8 aren't as dangerous as motorbikes.

6.2 A long way home page 40

Vocabulary family

1 1 *uncle*
   2 cousin
   3 son
   4 grandmother
   5 great-grandfather
   6 half-sister
   7 father-in-law
   8 niece
   9 stepfather

2 1 *couple*
   2 only child
   3 relatives
   4 get divorced
   5 twins
   6 single parent
   7 adopt
   8 get engaged

3 1 *single parent*
   2 grandfathers
   3 relatives
   4 uncles
   5 Couples
   6 get divorced
   7 only child
   8 daughters

4a 1 *adopt*
    2 parent
    3 divorced
    4 engaged
    5 only

Grammar present perfect simple and past simple

5 1 *My grandfather has given me his old car.*
   2 They haven't heard from their son this week.
   3 Has your friend ever spoken to her stepbrother?
   4 I've never met my cousins in Australia.
   5 My sister has found a new boyfriend.
   6 We haven't seen our great-grandparents recently.
   7 My mother-in-law has never invited us for a meal.
   8 Have you ever fallen down the stairs?

6 1 *lent*
   2 didn't enjoy
   3 haven't flown
   4 lived
   5 had
   6 've done
   7 went

7 1 *Have you ever done*
   2 I haven't travelled
   3 I've driven
   4 did you do
   5 My girlfriend gave
   6 did you go
   7 I didn't drive
   8 Did you enjoy
   9 Has she ever done
   10 She's climbed
   11 she's flown
   12 she hasn't jumped

6.3 Vocabulary development
page 42

Vocabulary adjective prefixes

1. *dis-*: dishonest, disorganized
   un-: *unfair*, unfriendly, unhappy, unhealthy, unkind, unlucky, unnecessary, unpleasant, unusual
   im-: impatient, impolite, impossible

2. 1 *unusual*
   2 impossible
   3 unhealthy
   4 dishonest
   5 impolite
   6 unpleasant
   7 disorganized
   8 unhappy

Vocabulary review

3. 1 *stupid*
   2 confident
   3 lazy
   4 sociable
   5 untidy

4. 1 *cousin*
   2 great-grandmother
   3 half-sister
   4 nephew
   5 couple
   6 get engaged
   7 relatives
   8 twins

5. 1 *disorganized*
   2 impolite
   3 unfriendly
   4 unhealthy
   5 unlucky
   6 unpleasant

6.4 Speaking and writing page 43

Writing responding to news on social media

1. 1 *I'm SO jealous!*
   2 Get well soon.
   3 Thinking of you.
   4 Good luck!
   5 You'll be fine.
   6 Well done!

2. 1 just
   2 already
   3 yet
   4 already

Speaking giving and responding to news

3. 1 *Guess what?*
   2 That's great news!
   3 I'm really happy for you.
   4 Oh no!
   5 Oh dear. I'm sorry.
   6 What a shame!
   7 Never mind.

4. **Conversation 1**
   A *Have you heard the news? About my sister and her husband?*
   B No. What?
   A They're adopting a baby.
   B How exciting! When are they getting him?
   A They're going to get him next month.
   B Oh wow! I can't wait to see him!

   Conversation 2
   A *I've got some bad news for you, Danny.*
   B What?
   A Tom and Alice are getting divorced.
   B That's terrible! What happened?
   A Tom moved out last week.
   B How awful! I'll call Alice tonight.

6.5 Reading for pleasure page 44

Little Rock

1. 2 racial

3. 1 *segregated*
   2 and black children wanted to go to Central High School
   3 break the law
   4 there were more protests outside Central High
   5 reacted to the situation
   6 by soldiers

Review: Units 5 and 6 page 45

Grammar

1. 1 *largest*   5 a
   2 any   6 Have
   3 went   7 more
   4 some

2. 1 *most*   5 many
   2 have   6 as
   3 a   7 lots
   4 the   8 been

Vocabulary

3. 1 *cash*
   2 adopt
   3 antique
   4 bank account
   5 engaged
   6 uncle
   7 divorced

4. 1 *ordinary*
   2 comfortable
   3 patient
   4 couple
   5 son
   6 quiet
   7 amount

5. 1 *unfriendly*
   2 stressful
   3 dishonest
   4 suitable
   5 disappointment
   6 possessions

Speaking

6. 1 *I've forgotten the word in English.*
   2 I'm really happy for you.
   3 Have you heard the news?
   4 That's what I'm looking for.
   5 You use it to open doors.

Unit 7 Travel
7.1 On the move page 46

Vocabulary transport

1. 1 c   4 a
   2 d   5 b
   3 e

2. 1 *greener*
   2 pollution
   3 crowded
   4 fuel
   5 reliable
   6 convenient
   7 fare

3. 1 *traffic jams*
   2 main roads
   3 public transport
   4 convenient
   5 fare
   6 reliable
   7 crowded
   8 greener

Grammar prediction (*will, might*)

4 1 'll be   4 'll park
   2 'll pass   5 'll rain
   3 'll have   6 'll win

5c 1 *quite sure*
   2 not very sure
   3 not very sure
   4 quite sure
   5 quite sure

6 1 'll   5 might
   2 might   6 'll
   3 might not   7 won't
   4 won't   8 might not

7 1 *will leave*
   2 will not (won't) see
   3 will be
   4 might not arrive
   5 will spend
   6 will not (won't) meet
   7 will feel
   8 will join
   9 will watch
   10 will be

7.2 Getting away page 48

Vocabulary holidays

1 1 *flight*
   2 accommodation
   3 souvenir
   4 insurance
   5 guidebook
   6 research
   7 culture
   8 reviews

2 1 *buy*   5 read
   2 lie   6 go
   3 get   7 experience
   4 try   8 explore

3 1 *book your flight*
   2 buy travel insurance
   3 hire a car
   4 choose your accommodation
   5 read online reviews
   6 apply for a visa

4a 1 book your flight
   2 lie by the pool
   3 try the local food
   4 hire a car
   5 read a guidebook
   6 apply for a visa
   7 go sightseeing
   8 explore the area

Grammar *something, anyone, everybody, nowhere,* etc.

5 1 *somewhere*
   2 something
   3 everywhere
   4 everybody / everyone
   5 nothing
   6 anything
   7 anybody / anyone
   8 nobody / no one

6 1 *somewhere*
   2 nowhere
   3 anything
   4 something
   5 everything
   6 Everybody
   7 anywhere
   8 No one

7.3 Vocabulary development page 50

Vocabulary *-ed* and *-ing* adjectives

1 1 ✓
   2 ✗ *embarrassing*
   3 ✗ disappointing
   4 ✗ excited
   5 ✓
   6 ✗ surprising
   7 ✓
   8 ✗ relaxed

2 1 *relaxing*
   2 annoyed
   3 tired
   4 fascinating
   5 embarrassed
   6 amazed
   7 boring
   8 confused

Vocabulary review

3 1 *road*   4 advance
   2 jams   5 transport
   3 pass

4 1 b   5 g
   2 f   6 c
   3 d   7 e
   4 a

5 1 *amazed* / ing
   2 bored / ing
   3 disappointed / ing
   4 excited / ing
   5 frightened / ing
   6 surprised / ing
   7 worried / ying

   8 annoyed / ing
   9 confused / ing
   10 embarrassed / ing
   11 fascinated / ing
   12 relaxed / ing

7.4 Speaking and writing page 51

Speaking checking into a hotel

1a 1 *Hi, I'd like to check in, please.*
   2 Yes, of course. Do you have a reservation?
   3 Yes, my name's Tatiana Genieva.
   4 OK, Ms Genieva. So that's a single room just for one night.
   5 Yeah, that's right.
   6 Could you fill in the registration form, please?
   7 Yeah, sure. Just one question. What time is check-out?
   8 You have to vacate your room by 10.30.
   9 Right. Is there anywhere I can leave my luggage tomorrow?
   10 Yes, you can leave it behind reception.
   11 Thanks a lot.

2 1 *Could we check in, please?*
   2 What was the name again, please?
   3 Is Wi-Fi available in the room?
   4 Is there a charge for it?
   5 I'll get someone to help you with your luggage.

Writing short notes and messages

3 1 *Thanks for your text. Am feeling much better.*
   2 Just left work. Want me to get some pizzas for dinner?
   3 Stuck in a traffic jam. Will be late for meeting.
   4 Lift out of order. Use stairs.
   5 See you at airport on Fri. Plane lands at 6.30.
   6 Am with client. Will call back in 15 mins.

Unit 8 Language and learning
8.1 The amazing human brain page 52

Grammar ability (*can, be able to*)

1a 1 *My sister isn't able to walk because she has broken her leg.*
   2 Are you able to lend me some money to go to a concert?
   3 I'm able to drive but I haven't got a car.

102

4 We're able to see the sea from the window of our room.
5 Is your partner able to speak any foreign languages?
6 I'm tired because I'm not able to sleep at night.

2
1 *can*
2 won't be able to
3 can
4 can't
5 won't be able to
6 can't

3
1 *can keep*
2 will be able to have
3 can't do
4 will be able to deal
5 be able to stop
6 won't be able to sleep
7 can make
8 will be able to phone
9 can relax
10 won't be able to go out

Vocabulary skills and abilities

4
++++ I'm brilliant
+++ I'm really good   I'm very good
++ I'm good
+ 'm OK I'm quite good
− I'm not very good
− − I'm terrible   I'm useless

5
1 *My girlfriend is quite good at making speeches.*
2 You're very good at telling jokes.
3 She's brilliant at organizing events.
4 I'm not very good at solving computer problems.
5 My husband is terrible at remembering people's names.
6 They're good at spelling.
7 I'm OK at following instructions.
8 We're useless at making decisions.
9 My daughter's really good at learning languages.
10 I'm useless at telling jokes.

6
1 *'s quite good at remembering*, 's useless at solving, 's very good at explaining   c
2 's good at organizing, isn't very good at learning, 's very good at making   b
3 's very good at understanding, 's OK at giving, 's really good at fixing   a
4 's quite good at following, 's terrible at telling, 's brilliant at taking   d

8.2 The secrets of a successful education page 54

Vocabulary & Speaking education

1
1 *drama*
2 languages
3 science
4 maths
5 economics
6 literature
7 physical
8 history
9 information
10 art

2
1 *take exams*
2 train
3 qualifications
4 Master's degree
5 relaxed
6 grades
7 psychology
8 state school
9 diploma

3
1 *private school*
2 strict
3 uniform
4 education
5 do well
6 success
7 degree
8 career

Grammar obligation, necessity and permission (*must, have to, can*)

4a
1 You can <u>use</u> the <u>internet</u>.
2 You <u>can't</u> <u>take</u> <u>photos</u>.
3 You can <u>sit</u> <u>here</u>.
4 You <u>can't</u> <u>walk</u> on the <u>grass</u>.
5 You can <u>pay</u> by <u>credit</u> <u>card</u>.
6 You <u>can't</u> <u>play</u> <u>football</u> <u>here</u>.

5
1 *don't have to*
2 *have to/must*
3 can
4 can't, mustn't
5 mustn't
6 have to
7 must, have to
8 can't

6
1 *has to give*
2 doesn't have to teach
3 has to / must prepare
4 mustn't / can't be
5 must / has to start
6 can't / mustn't relax
7 can get out
8 doesn't have to do

8.3 Vocabulary development page 56

Vocabulary *make* and *do*

1
1 *do*   5 make
2 make   6 doing
3 did   7 made
4 did   8 made

2
1 *do a course*
2 make a list
3 make your bed
4 make a salad
5 do nothing
6 make friends
7 do well
8 make a mistake
9 do housework

Vocabulary review

3
1 d   5 b
2 c   6 g
3 a   7 e
4 f

4
1 *brilliant*
2 terrible
3 really
4 good
5 OK

5
1 *art*
2 economics
3 IT, information technology
4 literature
5 PE, physical education
6 diploma
7 Master's degree
8 qualifications
9 success
10 uniform

6
1 *business*
2 an exam
3 homework
4 a job
5 well/badly
6 a decision
7 friends
8 a list
9 money
10 a phone call

8.4 Speaking and writing page 57

Speaking asking for clarification

1 1 c 4 b
   2 a 5 d
   3 e 6 f

2a 1 *Pardon*
   2 noisy in here
   3 breaking up
   4 could you speak up
   5 repeat that, please
   6 Please could you explain
   7 a really bad connection
   8 I'm a bit lost

Writing completing a form

3 1 *Title*
   2 Surname
   3 Forename
   4 Gender
   5 Date of birth
   6 Place of birth
   7 Marital status
   8 Occupation
   9 Next of kin
   10 Signature

8.5 Listening for pleasure page 58

Frightening experiences

1 1 *roundabout*
   2 landing
   3 snow
   4 fire
   5 passengers

3 1 *mother-in-law*
   2 snowing
   3 bike/bicycle
   4 lorry
   5 hotel
   6 fire
   7 plane
   8 land
   9 train
   10 (mobile) phone
   11 swimming
   12 panic
   13 son
   14 sister

Review 7 and 8 page 59

Grammar

1 1 *couldn't*
   2 might
   3 Everybody/Everyone
   4 will
   5 can't / mustn't
   6 anything
   7 able
   8 must

2 1 everywhere
   2 something
   3 can
   4 must
   5 will
   6 have
   7 might

Vocabulary

3 1 *crowded*
   2 learning languages
   3 buy souvenirs
   4 useless
   5 get foreign currency

4 1 *pollution*
   2 lie by the pool
   3 science
   4 trained
   5 greener
   6 fuel
   7 organizing events

5 1 *making*
   2 frightened
   3 embarrassing
   4 done
   5 make

Speaking

6 1 *Do you have a reservation?*
   2 Could we check in, please
   3 Could you fill in the registration form, please
   4 is Wi-Fi available in the room
   5 What do you mean by 'electronic device'

Unit 9 Body and mind

9.1 The rise and fall of the handshake page 60

Vocabulary body and actions

1 1 e   6 a
   2 j   7 f
   3 h   8 b
   4 d   9 c
   5 g   10 i

2 1 *forehead*
   2 cheek
   3 chin
   4 chest
   5 lip
   6 shoulder
   7 elbow
   8 thumb

3 1 *fist*   5 hug
   2 touch   6 elbows
   3 shake   7 nod
   4 cheek   8 smile

Grammar *if* + present simple, *will/won't/might*

4 1 *f*   5 d
   2 c   6 h
   3 a   7 e
   4 g   8 b

5 1 *tell*, won't say
   2 'll call, get
   3 Will you come, invite
   4 don't get up, won't have
   5 might get, finish
   6 Will you enjoy, doesn't go
   7 don't speak, might get
   8 'll be, go

7 1 *go*
   2 'll learn
   3 travel
   4 'll spend
   5 work
   6 'll have to
   7 find
   8 will be
   9 might feel
   10 don't go out
   11 won't meet
   12 stay
   13 practise
   14 'll feel

104

ANSWER KEY

9.2 Going back to nature page 62
Vocabulary health and fitness

1. 1 *weightlifting*
   2 viruses
   3 active
   4 cancer
   5 diet
   6 diseases
   7 stress

2. 1 *relax*
   2 junk food
   3 depressed
   4 gentle exercise
   5 illnesses
   6 Fitness
   7 natural food
   8 Cycling

3. 1 *natural food*
   2 diseases
   3 cancer
   4 diet
   5 junk food
   6 depressed
   7 active
   8 fitness

4a. 1 ✓ 5 ✓
    2 ✗ 6 ✓
    3 ✓ 7 ✗
    4 ✗ 8 ✓

Grammar present tenses in future time clauses

5. 1 *when*   4 if
   2 if   5 before
   3 after   6 as soon as

6. 1 *You'll be late if you don't hurry up.*
   2 I'll call you as soon as I get my results.
   3 We'll be disappointed if our daughter doesn't go to university.
   4 They'll go travelling after they finish their course.
   5 She'll talk to her boss before she makes a decision.
   6 We won't go to the party if we aren't invited.
   7 My son will learn to drive when he's 18.
   8 You won't get better if you don't practise.

7. 1 *will want*   5 starts
   2 go   6 sees
   3 doesn't have 7 don't like
   4 will tell   8 finishes

9.3 Vocabulary development page 64
Vocabulary verbs and prepositions

1. 1 *for*   4 of
   2 of   5 in
   3 on   6 to

2. 1 *belongs to*
   2 works for
   3 think of
   4 don't believe in
   5 depends on
   6 consists of
   7 succeeded in

Vocabulary review

3. 1 *clap*   6 chest
   2 hug   7 elbow
   3 nod   8 forehead
   4 shake   9 shoulder
   5 touch   10 tongue

4. 1 *cancer*   5 relax
   2 illnesses   6 diet
   3 active   7 natural food
   4 fitness   8 depressed

5. 1 *to*   6 to
   2 in   7 in
   3 of   8 of
   4 on   9 for
   5 of

9.4 Speaking and writing page 65
Speaking asking for help and giving advice

1. 1 *Hello. Please have a seat. Now, what can I do for you?*
   2 I've hurt my foot. I was playing football and I fell over.
   3 Let me have a look. It isn't broken, but I don't think you should walk on it.
   4 Yes, it hurts a lot. Could you give me something for the pain?
   5 Yes, I'll give you some painkillers. You could try putting ice on your foot, too.
   6 OK. How often should I take the tablets?
   7 It's one tablet with meals three times a day. And you mustn't do any sport for a week.
   8 Right. Thanks very much for your help.

2a. 1 *How can I help you?*
    2 Have you got anything
    3 I think you should
    4 you could try
    5 It's a good idea
    6 You mustn't

Writing a formal covering letter

3. 1 *Dear*
   2 wish
   3 enclose
   4 additional
   5 hear
   6 sincerely
   7 Madam
   8 like
   9 enclosed
   10 details
   11 hearing
   12 faithfully

Unit 10 Food
10.1 A question of taste page 66
Vocabulary describing food

1. ACROSS   DOWN
   2 *boiled* 1 plain
   4 snack   2 baked
   5 mild   3 hot
   6 stew   4 sweet
               6 sour

2. 1 *meal* made, raw – c
   2 sort, savoury, eat – a
   3 spices, tastes, served – d
   4 kind, bitter, has – b

3. 1 *herbs*   5 lamb
   2 Spicy   6 Dessert
   3 sauce   7 thick
   4 Fried   8 honey

4a. Two-syllable words: *chocolate*, different, favourite, raspberry, restaurant, several, strawberry
    Three-syllable words: interesting, temperature, vegetable

Grammar uses of the *-ing* form

5. 1 b   4 c
   2 a   5 f
   3 e   6 d

105

6
1 *buying* V
2 Having S
3 eating P
4 growing P
5 cooking V
6 Drinking S
7 making P
8 Heating S
9 inviting P

7
1 *going*   6 telling
2 eating   7 finishing
3 Trying   8 Knowing
4 preparing 9 serving
5 Getting

10.2 Canned dreams page 68

Vocabulary food containers

1

			B	O	X	
	J		O			
C	A	R	T	O	N	
	R		T	U	B	E
	C		L			
P	A	C	K	E	T	
	N			I		
				N		

2a
1 *tins*   5 jars
2 packets   6 boxes
3 bottles   7 cartons
4 tubes   8 cans

3
1 *jar*   5 tin
2 bottle   6 packet
3 box/packet   7 can/bottle
4 tube   8 carton

Grammar the passive

4
1 *drink*
2 didn't cook
3 were delivered
4 ate
5 aren't made
6 weren't invented
7 don't use
8 is produced

5
1 *Eggs are packed in boxes of six or twelve.*
2 Rice isn't grown in cold places.
3 This bread was baked yesterday.
4 Meals weren't eaten in front of the TV when I was young.
5 Milk wasn't sold in cartons in the past.
6 Toast is made with bread.
7 Those apple trees were planted last year.
8 Olives aren't usually served for dessert.

6
1 *are eaten*
2 was sold
3 wasn't bought
4 weren't added
5 is prepared
6 aren't used
7 were taken
8 isn't only served

10.3 Vocabulary development page 70

Vocabulary words with more than one meaning

1
1 *b*   5 a
2 b   6 b
3 a   7 a
4 a   8 a

2
1 diet
2 funny
3 past
4 left
5 mark

Vocabulary review

3
1 *baked*   6 mild
2 fried   7 savoury
3 honey   8 sweet
4 spices   9 sauce
5 bitter   10 stew

4
1 *d*   5 a
2 f   6 g
3 e   7 h
4 c   8 b

5
1 *bottle*   5 can
2 tube   6 tin
3 box   7 carton
4 jar   8 packet

6
1 *charge*   5 funny
2 clear   6 left
3 diet   7 mark
4 figure   8 past

10.4 Speaking and writing page 71

Speaking problems in a restaurant

1
1 *b*
2 a
3 c

2a Conversation 1
C Excuse me? I'm afraid I can't eat this steak. It's raw.
W Really? I'll take it back to the kitchen for you.
C No, I'd like to order something else, please.
W Of course. What would you like?
C I'm not sure. Would you mind bringing me the menu again?
W Of course not. I'm terribly sorry about your steak.
C Don't worry about it. Erm, I'll have a salad, please.

Conversation 2
C Excuse me? Could you possibly bring me the bill?
W Yes of course … Here it is.
C Oh. There seems to be a mistake.
W Is there?
C Yes. You've charged me for the steak, but I didn't eat it.
W You're absolutely right. I do apologize.
C Don't worry. It's not your fault.

Writing a restaurant review

3
1 ✓
2 ✗ *it hasn't been open for long.*
3 ✗ The owner's wife greeted us at the door.
4 ✗ The waiters were all very friendly.
5 ✓
6 ✗ My friends and I will definitely go back.
7 ✓
8 ✗ He's forgotten the drinks.

4
1 *location*
2 atmosphere
3 service
4 food
5 value for money

10.5 Reading for pleasure page 72

Making chocolate

1
1 b
2 d
3 a
4 c

3
1 *pods*   5 banana
2 three   6 tables
3 colour   7 brokers
4 boxes   8 factories

ANSWER KEY

Review: Units 9 and 10 page 73

Grammar

1 1 *is made*
    2 will have
    3 buying
    4 's
    5 doesn't rain
    6 eating
    7 start
    8 were taken

2 1 *Growing*
    2 won't see
    3 eating
    4 was started
    5 don't prepare
    6 are planted
    7 expecting
    8 begins

Vocabulary

3 1 *fist*
    2 depressed
    3 herbs
    4 forehead
    5 active
    6 tongue
    7 dessert
    8 stress

4 1 *savoury* 5 carton
    2 stew 6 tin
    3 lamb 7 bottle
    4 spicy 8 tube

5 1 *mark* 5 in
    2 of 6 funny
    3 diet 7 to
    4 on 8 left

Speaking

6 1 *I think you should stay in bed.*
    2 Could you possibly give me a clean plate?
    3 You mustn't lift anything heavy.
    4 There seems to be a mistake in the bill.
    5 Have you got anything for a sore throat?
    6 You could try putting some cream on it.

Unit 11 World

11.1 Making the world a better place page 74

Vocabulary global issues

1 1 e 6 c
    2 f 7 b
    3 i 8 h
    4 a 9 d
    5 g

2 1 *factory* 6 cure
    2 create 7 crisis
    3 global 8 spread
    4 figures 9 hunger
    5 happiness

3 1 *global*
    2 environment
    3 facts
    4 factories
    5 warming
    6 health
    7 hunger
    8 situation
    9 financial
    10 unemployment

Grammar if + past tense + would

4a 1 *If I had a car, I would drive to work.*
    2 I wouldn't be happy if I lost my job.
    3 What would you do if you could go back in time?
    4 If she knew his number, she'd call him.
    5 Where would you live if you had the choice?
    6 You'd feel better if you did some exercise.

4c 2 I wouldn't be happy if I lost my job.
    3 What would you do if you could go back in time?
    4 If she knew his number, she'd call him.
    5 Where would you live if you had the choice?
    6 You'd feel better if you did some exercise.

5 1 *worked, would have*
    2 wouldn't leave, wasn't
    3 would … go, had
    4 wouldn't be, didn't get up
    5 'd have, lived
    6 didn't rain, wouldn't grow
    7 'd enjoy, didn't work
    8 would … say, met

6 1 *would happen*
    2 would … be
    3 became
    4 wouldn't need
    5 would … go
    6 didn't eat

11.2 Breaking news page 76

Grammar used to

1a 1 *My brother used to work in a bank.*
    2 We didn't use to have a garden.
    3 My parents used to live in a flat.
    4 Did you use to have long hair?
    5 I didn't use to drink coffee.
    6 Did your boyfriend use to have a motorbike?
    7 I used to wear glasses.

2 1 ✓
    2 ✗ *We didn't use to do anything at weekends, but now we go walking.*
    3 ✗ What kind of music did you use to listen to when you were a teenager?
    4 ✓
    5 ✗ One day, we had a car accident.
    6 ✗ They didn't use to eat fish, but now they prefer it to meat.
    7 ✗ Our children didn't use to go out at night, but now they do.

3 1 *Did … use to watch*
    2 used to be
    3 didn't use to work
    4 used to look
    5 didn't use to smile
    6 didn't use to happen
    7 used to read
    8 used to sit

Vocabulary the news

4 1 *hurricane* 4 forest fire
    2 election 5 flood
    3 strike 6 robbery

107

5 1 *articles*
   2 crash
   3 Journalists
   4 natural disaster
   5 reach
   6 report
   7 social media
   8 spread
   9 up to date
   10 weekly

6 1 *natural disasters*
   2 reach
   3 Journalists
   4 report
   5 social media
   6 spread
   7 articles
   8 up to date
   9 weekly
   10 crash

11.3 Vocabulary development
page 78

Vocabulary phrasal verbs

1 1 *take up*   5 put down
   2 find out   6 give up
   3 put on   7 set up
   4 grow up

2 1 *When did you find them out?*
   2 I'm giving them up.
   3 He put it down on the platform.
   4 When did you set it up?
   5 If you're cold, put them on.
   6 Why have you taken it up?

Vocabulary review

3 1 *technology*
   2 economic
   3 Facts
   4 farming
   5 warming
   6 wellbeing
   7 increasing
   8 hunger

4 1 *articles*
   2 report
   3 journalists
   4 social media
   5 natural disasters
   6 weekly

5 1 *on*   5 down
   2 out   6 on
   3 up   7 up
   4 up   8 up

11.4 Speaking and writing page 79

Speaking expressing and responding to opinions

1a 1 *think*   5 point
    2 view   6 right
    3 agree   7 Personally
    4 True   8 Maybe

2 1 *I agree*
   2 In my opinion
   3 I disagree
   4 I don't have
   5 Yeah, but
   6 I don't think
   7 a good point

Writing a presentation

3 1 *tell your friends your password.*
   2 networks are not 100% safe.
   3 not accept friend requests from strangers.
   4 chat with your real friends.
   5 not post (your) holiday dates on Facebook.
   6 log off social media before you leave the room.

Unit 12 Work

12.1 The working environment
page 80

Vocabulary jobs, professions and workplaces

1 1 *construction*
   2 building site
   3 judge
   4 law
   5 nurse
   6 hospital
   7 personal assistant
   8 office
   9 medical research
   10 laboratory

2 1 *developer*
   2 factory
   3 journalist
   4 Engineering
   5 administrator
   6 scientist
   7 accountant
   8 Sales

3 1 c   4 e
   2 d   5 a
   3 b   6 f

4 1 *scientists*
   2 laboratory
   3 medical
   4 office
   5 hospital
   6 nurse
   7 accountant
   8 health care

Grammar present perfect simple with *for* and *since*

5a 1 *My father has had his car for too long.*
    2 Those children have studied English since last year.
    3 My wife has liked the same music since she was a student.
    4 My parents have been married for 30 years.
    5 John has worked as a teacher since he left university.
    6 My friends have lived in Scotland for six months.

6 1 *have you had your current job? I've had my current job for seven years.*
   2 has your sister lived abroad? She's lived abroad for three months.
   3 long have your parents worked in engineering? They've worked in engineering since they were young.
   4 How long have you known your best friend? I've known my best friend for ages.
   5 How long has your partner been a software developer? He's been a software developer since he left university.
   6 How long has your daughter played the guitar? She's played the guitar since last year.

7 1 *has loved, since*
   2 has had, for
   3 has used, for
   4 hasn't spoken, since
   5 has been, for
   6 has wanted, since

12.2 The changing face of work
page 82

Vocabulary job responsibilities

1 1 *do*
   2 train

ANSWER KEY

3 give
4 entertain
5 run
6 recruit
7 employ
8 attend

2   1 *team*
    2 staff
    3 paperwork
    4 clients
    5 meetings
    6 enquiries
    7 presentations
    8 business
    9 emails

3   1 *recruit*
    2 works in
    3 are attending/attend
    4 give
    5 writes
    6 advise
    7 talking on
    8 deal with

Grammar uses of the infinitive with *to*

4   1 e   4 c
    2 f   5 a
    3 b   6 d

5a 1 *to work*
    2 to celebrate
    3 not to say
    4 not to tell
    5 to talk
    6 not to worry
    7 not to call
    8 to take

6   1 *to have*   5 to go
    2 to attend   6 to do
    3 to open   7 to return
    4 to get   8 to give

12.3 Vocabulary development
page 84

Vocabulary phrases with *in*

1   1 *in construction*
    2 in common
    3 in trouble
    4 in a suit
    5 in charge of
    6 in five minutes' time
    7 in a hurry
    8 in a mess
    9 in the middle of
    10 in detail

Vocabulary review

2   1 *administrator* 2 judge 3 scientist
    4 engineering 5 law 6 sales 7 court
    8 hospital 9 office

3   1 *clients*
    2 enquiries
    3 the phone
    4 meetings
    5 staff
    6 presentations
    7 a team

4   1 *in detail*
    2 in common
    3 in ten minutes
    4 in the middle
    5 in nursing
    6 in sales
    7 in a suit
    8 in shorts

12.4 Speaking and writing page 85

Writing a curriculum vitae (CV)

1   1 e   5 h
    2 d   6 c
    3 f   7 a
    4 b   8 g

2   1 *managed*
    2 training
    3 developed
    4 attended
    5 provided
    6 assisted
    7 fluent
    8 basic
    9 knowledge
    10 request

Speaking answering questions in a job interview

3a 1 've got a university degree
    2 I've worked as a
    3 I'm currently working for
    4 I'd really like to get into
    5 I'm good at
    6 I can
    7 I find it hard to

12.5 Listening for pleasure page 86

Easter Island statues

1   1 c   2 a   3 b

3   1 *887*
    2 trees

3 easy
4 make statues
5 transport
6 trees

Review: Units 11 and 12 page 87

Grammar

1   1 *to arrive*
    2 looked after
    3 phone
    4 have had
    5 to stop
    6 would buy

2   1 *if*   5 since
    2 would   6 have
    3 use   7 to
    4 used   8 not

Vocabulary

3   1 *journalist*   4 report
    2 reach   5 recruit
    3 cure   6 judge

4   1 *unemployment*
    2 Advances
    3 construction
    4 software developers
    5 health care
    6 nurses
    7 administration
    8 paperwork

5   1 *grow up*
    2 in charge of
    3 in common
    4 carry on
    5 in a mess
    6 find out

Speaking

6   1 *I'm sorry, but I don't really agree.*
    2 I'm currently working for an IT company.
    3 I'd really like to get into sales.
    4 In my opinion, world hunger should not exist.
    5 I don't have strong views on the media.
    6 I find it hard to work in a team.

109

Irregular verbs

Infinitive	Past simple	Past participle
be	was/were	been
become	became	become
begin	began	begun
break	broke	broken
bring	brought	brought
build	built	built
buy	bought	bought
can	could	been able to
catch	caught	caught
choose	chose	chosen
come	came	come
cost	cost	cost
cut	cut	cut
do	did	done
drink	drank	drunk
drive	drove	driven
eat	ate	eaten
fall	fell	fallen
feel	felt	felt
fight	fought	fought
find	found	found
fly	flew	flown
forget	forgot	forgotten
freeze	froze	frozen
get	got	got
give	gave	given
go	went	gone/been
grow	grew	grown
have	had	had
hear	heard	heard
hit	hit	hit
keep	kept	kept
know	knew	known
learn	learnt/learned	learnt/learned
leave	left	left

Infinitive	Past simple	Past participle
lend	lent	lent
let	let	let
lose	lost	lost
make	made	made
meet	met	met
pay	paid	paid
put	put	put
read	read	read
ride	rode	ridden
ring	rang	rung
run	ran	run
say	said	said
see	saw	seen
sell	sold	sold
send	sent	sent
shut	shut	shut
sing	sang	sung
sit	sat	sat
sleep	slept	slept
speak	spoke	spoken
spend	spent	spent
stand	stood	stood
steal	stole	stolen
swim	swam	swum
take	took	taken
teach	taught	taught
tell	told	told
think	thought	thought
throw	threw	thrown
understand	understood	understood
wake	woke	woken
wear	wore	worn
win	won	won
write	wrote	written

Phonemic symbols

Single vowel sounds

/iː/	tree /triː/	/ə/	computer /kəmˈpjuːtə(r)/
/ɪ/	his /hɪz/	/ɜː/	learn /lɜːn/
/i/	happy /ˈhæpi/	/ɔː/	four /fɔː(r)/
/ʊ/	good /gʊd/	/æ/	hat /hæt/
/u/	usual /ˈjuːʒuəl/	/ʌ/	sunny /ˈsʌni/
/uː/	school /skuːl/	/ɑː/	car /kɑː(r)/
/e/	ten /ten/	/ɒ/	clock /klɒk/

Diphthongs (double vowel sounds)

/ɪə/	near /nɪə(r)/	/ɔɪ/	boy /bɔɪ/
/ʊə/	tour /tʊə(r)/	/aɪ/	try /traɪ/
/eə/	wear /weə(r)/	/əʊ/	so /səʊ/
/eɪ/	train /treɪn/	/aʊ/	out /aʊt/

Consonant sounds

/p/	pen /pen/	/s/	see /siː/
/b/	big /bɪg/	/z/	lazy /ˈleɪzi/
/t/	tea /tiː/	/ʃ/	shower /ˈʃaʊə(r)/
/d/	do /duː/	/ʒ/	television /ˈtelɪvɪʒn/
/tʃ/	children /ˈtʃɪldrən/	/m/	man /mæn/
/dʒ/	journey /ˈdʒɜːni/	/n/	never /ˈnevə(r)/
/k/	cat /kæt/	/ŋ/	sing /sɪŋ/
/g/	go /gəʊ/	/h/	hot /hɒt/
/f/	fly /flaɪ/	/l/	like /laɪk/
/v/	very /ˈveri/	/r/	river /ˈrɪvə(r)/
/θ/	thing /θɪŋ/	/w/	water /ˈwɔːtə(r)/
/ð/	this /ðɪs/	/j/	yes /jes/

OXFORD
UNIVERSITY PRESS

Great Clarendon Street, Oxford, OX2 6DP, United Kingdom

Oxford University Press is a department of the University of Oxford.
It furthers the University's objective of excellence in research, scholarship,
and education by publishing worldwide. Oxford is a registered trade
mark of Oxford University Press in the UK and in certain other countries

© Oxford University Press 2015

The moral rights of the author have been asserted

First published in 2015

2020 2019 2018

10 9 8 7 6 5 4 3

No unauthorized photocopying

All rights reserved. No part of this publication may be reproduced, stored
in a retrieval system, or transmitted, in any form or by any means, without
the prior permission in writing of Oxford University Press, or as expressly
permitted by law, by licence or under terms agreed with the appropriate
reprographics rights organization. Enquiries concerning reproduction outside
the scope of the above should be sent to the ELT Rights Department, Oxford
University Press, at the address above

You must not circulate this work in any other form and you must impose
this same condition on any acquirer

Links to third party websites are provided by Oxford in good faith and for
information only. Oxford disclaims any responsibility for the materials
contained in any third party website referenced in this work

ISBN: 978 0 19 456544 8

Printed in China

This book is printed on paper from certified and well-managed sources

ACKNOWLEDGEMENTS

The publisher would like to thank the following for permission to reproduce photographs:
Alamy Images pp.5 (women/Ken Weingart), 7 (nightclub/Lou Linwei), 9 (tea leaf/yu liang wong), 12 (Gojohaven/Horizons WWP), 15 (colleagues/PhotoAlto), 16 (wastewater pipes/Robert Brook), 17 (Egypt cruise ship/Hemis), 19 (Yuri Gagarin/Heritage Image Partnership Ltd), 27 (Pregnant woman/Stockbroker), 27 (Plane taking off/Eric Gevaert), 30 (Semi detached house/Paul Thompson Images), 31 (Houdini/Mary Evans Picture Library), 32 (old TV/Judith Collins), 32 (plasma TV/Tony Cordoza), 34 (bill/D. Hurst), 34 (credit card/incamerastock), 37 (couple shopping/Kzenon), 38 (women in burqa/Alan Gignoux), 40 (smiling woman/MBI), 40 (brother & sister/Wave Royalty Free/Design Pics Inc), 41 (male driver/Denis Rozhnovsky), 45 (Aung San Suu Kyi/Homer Sykes), 47 (Mars/PF-(space1)), 55 (elevator/Dinodia Photos), 57 (woman at club/ImageDB), 65 (pharmacist/Blend Images), 72 (cacao fruit/Bon Appetit), 79 (chatting/Bill Lyons), 81 (Professor Stephen Hawking), 83 (woman with plaster/Radius Images), 86 (Easter Island/M. Timothy O'Keefe), 86 (Moai statues/John Elk III); Corbis p.13 (kitchen/Justin Paget/Tetra Images); Getty Images pp.7 (exercise class/Blake Little), 13 (towel/sinankocaslan), 13 (dirty dish cloth/Erkki Makkonen), 13 (wardrobe/Richard Wheatley), 22 (jogging/SelectStock), 24 (Bill Gates/Chesnot), 25 (Tired woman in office/Bodil Johansson), 27 (Skydiver/Joe McBride), 27 (Couple shopping/LdF), 27 (Groom checking watch/Brand X Pictures), 27 (Couple waking to tennis courts/Image Source), 28 (Wedding ring exchange/Eric Larrayadieu), 29 (El Prado Museum/PNC), 33 (Voyager 1/The LIFE Picture Collection), 42 (eccentric woman/Chris Aschenbrener), 51 (check in/Shalom Ormsby), 53 (speaker/Ghislain & Marie David de Lossy), 54 (Indian schoolchildren/AFP), 58 (roundabout/James Morgan), 58 (snowy road/Tetra Images-Johannes Kroemer), 58 (on a train/Westend61), 61 (flatmates/Franek Strzeszewski), 68 (Loren Shriver/Space Frontiers), 76 (female anchor/ColorBlind Images), 82 (water slide/Justin Lewis); iStockphoto pp.13 (carpet/zxcynosure), 13 (mirror/emesilva), 13 (clothesline/MartynaPiorek), 13 (duvet/NAKphotos); Oxford University Press pp.16 (cover), 34 (ten dollars/Westend61), 44 (cover), 50 (Eiffel Tower/Eike Van de Velde), 72 (cover), 85 (PE/Gareth Boden); Press Association Images pp.21 (Larry Walters/Randy Mudrick/AP), 44 (Civil Rights Integration 1957/William p. Straeter/AP); Shutterstock pp.4 (jogger/wavebreakmedia), 7 (basketball/AstroStar), 7 (woman on laptop/Aaron Amat), 7 (gym/wavebreakmedia), 7 (playing cards/racorn), 7 (yoga/East), 7 (camping/wavebreakmedia), 10 (Marrakesh/Kemal Taner), 11 (Barcelona/Liudmila Ermolenko), 18 (bull/Stefanie Mohr Photography), 19 (earth/Denis Tabler), 20 (sad boy/RimDream), 23 (stuck car/Piotr Sikora), 34 (wallet/mrHanson), 34 (purse/Timof), 34 (bag/Elnur), 35 (parking meter/Dmitry Kalinovsky), 39 (fruit salad/margouillat photo), 46 (Mayakovskaya metro station/d13), 48 (shopping/emberiza), 49 (Krakow/De Visu), 53 (mechanic/wavebreakmedia), 53 (class/Monkey Business Images), 53 (doctor/pkchai), 58 (airplane/Ondrej Zabransky), 58 (fire/James Steidl), 60 (man/Kiko Calderon ESP), 62 (veg/cooperr), 63 (stretching/Robert Kneschke), 64 (open living room/smoxx), 66 (zucchini tart/zi3000), 66 (tiramisu/cobraphotography), 66 (sushi/Ostancov Vladislav), 66 (green curry/Sommai), 67 (chef/wavebreakmedia), 69 (pizza/svry), 70 (tomato/S-F), 70 (garlic.Peter Zijlstra), 70 (cucumber/Gosia McCurdy), 70 (onions/S1001), 71 (fish icon/Anthonycz), 74 (refinery/Kodda), 75 (cow/Sebastian Knight), 77 (tropical storm/B747), 77 (voting/Ververidis Vasilis), 77 (protest/Eric Crama), 77 (forest fire/Ruslan Absurdov), 77 (flood/paintings), 77 (theft/Syda Productions), 78 (kayaking/kuznetcov_konstantin), 84 (cement/Zurijeta).

Cover image by: Getty Images/teekid

The authors and publisher are grateful to those who have given permission to reproduce the following extracts and adaptations of copyright material:

p16 Extract from Oxford Bookworms Library 3: *Chemical Secret* by Tim Vicary © Oxford University Press 2008. Reproduced by permission.

p44 Extract from Oxford Bookworms Library 3 Factfile: *Martin Luther King* by Alan McLean © Oxford University Press 2008. Reproduced by permission.

p72 Extract from Oxford Bookworms Library 2 Factfile: *Chocolate* by Janet Hardy-Gould © Oxford University Press 2011. Reproduced by permission.

Sources:
http://www.huffingtonpost.ca
http://www.centerparcs.co.uk